Praise for *Jesus and the Abolitionists*

"This is a book, at once, of love and radicality. Stokes offers a unique voice into the ways Christianity and the teachings of Jesus necessitate an anarchist worldview. There is a forthright demand, via a Christian ethic of love, to renounce the violence and domination of the state, while simultaneously creating something more loving, more caring. Indeed, I felt loved reading this book, reading of Stokes's life, of the beautifully necessary entanglement of Christianity and anarchism. And in that love, I felt radicalized. And you will too. I promise."

—**Marquis Bey,** professor at Northwestern University and author of *Anarcho-Blackness*

"*Jesus and the Abolitionists* hums with freedom. Terry Stokes testifies to a robust vision of an anarchist future grounded in Black experience—a future both practical and realizable. Stokes introduces readers to political life beyond coercion and to a faith outside the reaches of violence. Weaving together political theory, scriptural insight, and theological rigor, Stokes's accessible book is a gift to anyone who has looked at a world devastated by the vapidity of statecraft and wondered, 'Is there another way?'"

—**Melissa Florer-Bixler,** pastor of Raleigh Mennonite Church

"*Jesus and the Abolitionists* offers a practical, systematic theology for Christians who seek to live generously, lovingly, and compassionately in a world marked by division. Stokes's call is wonderfully local, drawing the reader into the public to serve their neighbor. This anarchic vision is one of building, not burning—of asking hard questions while also proposing how we might live with Christlike, communal focus on God's redemptive work. For those seeking an innovative, creative engagement with the Christian practice in our world today, this is a worthwhile read."

—**Amar D. Peterman**, founder, Scholarship for Religion and Society

"Terry Stokes challenges the mundanity of Western Christian communities in vivid and provoking ways. I came away from this work stirred, challenged, and charged."

—**Rev. Solomon Missouri**, pastor of Invitation AME Zion Church, Snow Hill, NC

"In *Jesus and the Abolitionists*, Stokes employs wisdom and humor to ignite a brilliant ethical and biblical imagination. This book is a necessary text for Christians who feel called to participate in justice movements, because it recognizes the reality of history while offering a vision for our future when and where justice is possible. *Jesus and the Abolitionists* provides abundant hope, which is as much a balm as a fuel, nourishing us and calling us into a new way."

—**Erin Jean Warde**, author of *Sober Spirituality: The Joy of a Mindful Relationship with Alcohol*

Jesus and the Abolitionists

JESUS AND THE
ABOLITIONISTS

HOW ANARCHIST
CHRISTIANITY EMPOWERS
THE PEOPLE

Terry J. Stokes

Broadleaf Books

Minneapolis

Library of Congress Cataloging-in-Publication Data

Names: Stokes, Terry J., author.
Title: Jesus and the abolitionists : how anarchist Christianity empowers
  the people / Terry Jonathan Stokes.
Description: Minneapolis : Broadleaf Books, [2024] | Includes
  bibliographical references.
Identifiers: LCCN 2023039836 (print) | LCCN 2023039837 (ebook) | ISBN
  9798889830818 (print) | ISBN 9798889830825 (ebook)
Subjects: LCSH: Christian anarchism.
Classification: LCC HX833 .S75 2024 (print) | LCC HX833 (ebook) | DDC
  335/.83—dc23/eng/20231101
LC record available at https://lccn.loc.gov/2023039836
LC ebook record available at https://lccn.loc.gov/2023039837

Cover design: Carlos Esparza

Print ISBN: 979-8-8898-3081-8
eBook ISBN: 979-8-8898-3082-5

Printed in China.

contents

acknowledgments

I owe the genesis of my anarchist exodus to Nobuko, who piqued my interest by telling me about her anarchist friends and their love for mutual aid.

I am grateful to Terry, June, and Jaclyn, who bore with me as I wrote most of the first draft of this book in the back seat as we drove throughout the state of Texas together. To live with your unconditional love and support is to come to believe that God's power, working in us, can do infinitely more than we can ask or imagine. You, my beloved family, have made all things possible for me—from authorship to anarchy. In a way, this is all your doing. ☺

I am grateful to Alyssa, who patiently—and excitedly!—listened to me talk about anarchism on our first date and even followed up by researching the anarchy of Swiss mountain cantons.

I am grateful to David, who has been not only a dear friend but also a consistent philosophical and theological interlocutor.

preface

Christian radicalism—which, it could be argued, is a redundant phrase—
is a rich, robust historical tradition. From St. John the Revelator to
St. Moses the Ethiopian, from St. Julian of Norwich to St. Francis of
Assisi, from Frederick Douglass to W. E. B. Du Bois, from Howard
Thurman to Fannie Lou Hamer, the line is long and unbroken.

Each generation, however, has to build on the work of the
former and articulate the vision anew in the language of the times.
As I progressed on my own journey of radicalization, I found many
beautiful such articulations—christian arguments for Black liberation, christian arguments for abolition of prisons and police, christian arguments for socialism, and so on. What I would like to do here,
in a rudimentary, expressly nonacademic, and lighthearted way, is to
propose a *system* of christian radicalism. I would like to offer a set
of radical theological beliefs that cohere, have an internal binding
logic, and demonstrate—but not exhaust—a comprehensiveness of
thought. I hope that my social location—as a Black millennial lay
theologian—affords me a voice and vantage point that can offer
something special to this ongoing tradition.

Let me quickly say that I am not attempting to *fuse* christianity
and anarchism in this book. Spirituality and political philosophy are
two different disciplines with different methods, purposes, fields of
inquiry, and kinds of conclusions. What I *am* attempting to do, rather,

is to demonstrate that christianity necessarily leads to anarchy. Why? Because the ethical teachings of Jesus—namely, nonviolence, cooperation, and love—demand the immediate renunciation of the inherently violent and domineering state, as well as the construction of something else in its place. So while I expressly *reject* the idea that one must be a christian in order to be an anarchist,[1] I do believe that christianity is—intrinsically and necessarily—one of several spiritual and philosophical pathways to an anarchist worldview.

And the teachings of Jesus don't merely lead to anarchism in some abstract, ultimate, at-some-point-in-the-future way. They demand an anarchist ethic immediately. Why? Well, for one, they're based on what his tradition claims about the inherent nature of God and humankind and not merely the *telos* (the ultimate end) of humanity. Therefore, consent to the state and all institutions that operate explicitly or implicitly by violence, including law, courts, police, and prisons, is not a concession that we must make to a not yet fully remade world but rather a moral failure that we must immediately reject if we are to be faithful to Christ here and now. In light of this, the claims that christianity makes about spirituality and the claims anarchism makes about political organization are both ethically resonant and practically reinforcing.

Let me also note here that this is not a composite work. It is one person's original[2] construction of an *anarchist christianity*—note which

---

1. Which unfortunately seems to be the premise of much that is termed *christian anarchism*, as if the anarchy in which society and the church have melded into one, and everyone is christian, is the truest or only real anarchism, which I fully reject.
2. *Original* not in the sense that I am presenting ideas that no one else ever has but rather that the origin of the particular constructive work I do here between christianity and anarchism is in me rather than anyone else (i.e., if Twitter has proved anything, it's that two different people can come up with similar thoughts independently of one another).

word is modifying which—based on my own understanding of anarchism and my own understanding of christianity. This is a theological and philosophical manifesto rather than an academic review of a field of study.[3]

I am a nonacademic lay theologian. I am a professional in the sense that it is my vocation to theologize but not in the sense that I belong to the "guild" of theologians that has its locus in the academy. As such, this work will seek to be popular in outlook and tone while also being theologically rigorous. We are definitely going to get after it intellectually, but I hope all of it is relevant and accessible.

You know how a child will draw their parent, or grandparent, or sibling and then give them the drawing, and their family member will be so unbelievably happy and proud of what the child has done? Artistically the drawing may need work, but the fact that this young child put effort and creativity into their own take on what their family looks like, and all that this represents in terms of their development and identity, is powerful. That's what I hope this book might be. A little child trying to draw a big God and doing a job that is hopelessly limited but, perhaps, subjectively beautiful. And pleasing to God. And hopefully encouraging to you.

---

3. If you *are* looking for a composite work, I recommend Christoyannapolous's *Christian Anarchism*, which is listed in the further reading section.

Part One: Anarchism

When will you tire of such a civilization and declare in words . . . "Away with a civilization that thus degrades me; it is not worth the saving?"

—Lucy Parsons[1]

---

1. Lucy Parsons, "Our Civilization: Is it Worth Saving?" *The Alarm* (August 8, 1885); Gale Ahrens, ed., *Lucy Parsons: Freedom, Equality, and Solidarity; Writings and Speeches, 1878–1937* (Chicago: Charles H. Kerr Revolutionary Classics, 2003).

One

the past's politic
my journey to anarchism

where I come from

It's the late 1960s. Maurice White is leaving the Ramsey Lewis Trio to start a group called Earth, Wind and Fire. Carlos Santana is about to invent Latin rock at Woodstock. The musical revolutions are outdone only by social revolution. People are out here getting radicalized. And two cuties are growing up on opposite sides of the Hampton Roads Bridge-Tunnel—757, baby. If you know, you know.

One of them spends his early childhood racing paper boats in the gutters of the projects on rainy days. The other comes home to Virginia after being stationed on a military base in West Germany and summering in Switzerland. One spends sunday mornings bouncing on his mama's lap at Queen Street Baptist Church while the choir sings a cappella. The other buttons up at an ecumenical liturgical church on base. One thing they both do is pull off the incredible feat of joining one of the first cohorts of Black engineers at Virginia Tech. They were actually in their last year there when Steph Curry's parents were in their first year, but tragically, they did *not* have the chance to befriend them and make them my eventual godparents (no disrespect to my actual godparents—I love you!).

My mother was raised in a Black liberal bourgeois family, while my father was raised in a Black working-class family.

My paternal grandfather was a W. E. B. Du Bois radical, and my paternal grandmother was a Booker T. Washington conservative. Many people do not know that Du Bois was a onetime member of the Communist Party (USA), and his greatest work was a Marxist interpretation of the period of Reconstruction. On the other hand, Booker T's message was essentially "keep your head down, work hard, and you might be able to join the capitalists." For him there was no sense in (or need for) directly confronting or trying to undo the underlying structures of racism and capitalism.

So my father encountered two very different political worldviews from each of his parents, but the radical one came from the words and actions of an emotionally unavailable father, while the conservative one came from a precious, adorable, salt-of-the-earth mother. You can probably guess which way he ended up leaning himself. He also ended up going to, you guessed it, Booker T. Washington High School.

It's not surprising that my grandmother was team Booker T. Most southern Black folk of her generation were. Du Bois himself said as much: "This brings us to the situation when Booker T. Washington became the leader of the Negro race and advised them to depend upon industrial education and work rather than politics."[1]

My mother's father is a second-generation Tuskegee Airman. He spent twenty years in the US Air Force and then spent another twenty as an administrator with NASA; he actually worked with

---

1.   W. E. B. Du Bois, *Black Reconstruction in America, 1860–1880* (New York: Free Press, 1998), 694.

Katherine Johnson of *Hidden Figures* fame. My mother's mother was an educator—a teacher and then a principal and then a school administrator. She is the only one of my relatives I know to have earned a doctorate (as a Black woman in the mid-twentieth century, at that). My maternal grandparents met at Howard University, a historically Black college/university known for producing some of the best liberal Black minds in US history. They joined Black fraternities and sororities—Alpha Phi Omega and Kappa Delta Pi—got great jobs and put together successful professional careers, joined civic clubs, and went on to live upwardly mobile lives. We're talking about brunch at the officers' club *every* sunday, a house that trick-or-treaters loudly proclaimed to be a mansion, scholarship funds in our name, a pool table upstairs, name-brand everything, *Black and Bougie*™ everything.

So my father was a Booker T. conservative, and my mother was a self-described "flaming liberal" when the two of them met in college. My father was the first in his family to go to a four-year college, while my mother was one in a long line of college attendees, from whom a degree was expected. They both had life-changing experiences with evangelical christianity in college. The Jesus movement, one of those revolutions from the late 1960s, was enjoying a prominent afterlife in campus fellowship groups across the country. Revivals right after intramurals. Altar calls right after algebra—well, differential equations, but that's not as alliterative. Large-group services featuring relatable teaching and the latest bangers from Amy Grant and Darlene Zschech. (Sing along if you know it! SHOUT TO THE LORD, ALL THE EARTH, LET US SING / POWER AND MAJESTY, PRAISE TO THE KING.) Small group Bible studies that made the scriptures come alive for the first time since third-grade sunday school. Which is all wonderful until you open up the hood and realize it's all been made into one component of the engine of the religious right. So in the midst of a life-affirming spiritual awakening, my father's Black conservatism was interwoven with white evangelical conservatism, and my mother's Black liberalism was challenged and eventually replaced by a conservatism cocktail akin to my father's.

my journey

Because of these histories, I was raised in a conservative evangelical household.[2] I grew up with a lot of wonderful ideas, as well as some harmful political and sociological ideas such as meritocracy—the ones who succeed do so by their merit; the bootstrap mentality—the ones who succeed do so because they work hard; and, of course, capitalism as the system best designed to shape "natural" human self-centeredness into a society where everyone can work hard and succeed.

My worldview was challenged in college but not much, even though I was at a school with a very liberal reputation. There was some significant Black liberation organizing that happened on campus during my fourth year, which did act as an awakening moment for me, but I was not properly radicalized until much later.

My time in seminary was the real genesis of my move toward radicalism. It was the first progressive christian space I'd ever inhabited. All of a sudden, I was confronted with women pastors, LGBTQ+ theologians, and a host of people and experiences that forced me to examine my beliefs about gender and sexuality, which led to even more fundamental questions about God, divine revelation, and

---

2. While my political visions diverge from those of some of my elders and ancestors, I hold empathy for how they arrived at their views, and I am deeply grateful to them for often doing their best to pursue love and liberation with the resources available to them. I disagree with many, but I judge no one, and I seek to honor and love everyone—especially my parents. I love you, Mom and Dad!

christian ethics. As I went into my third and final year there in the fall of 2019, I felt that I was finally emerging from a time of severe cognitive dissonance into a time of intellectual cohesion and spiritual clarity, which felt wonderful. I now considered myself part of the inclusive orthodoxy community of folks who enthusiastically assent to the apostles and Nicene Creeds *and* believe that the life of the church is expressly for all people, and its leadership is accessible to all and not qualified by gender or sexuality.

And then we entered the year of our Lord 2020, which made me a leftist. That iteration of the Black liberation movement, alongside the revelation of inequities laid bare by the pandemic, turned me into an abolitionist. I became someone who believes that many societal institutions, especially but not exclusively police and prisons, need to be completely deconstructed and replaced with new institutions designed for justice, inclusion, and equity.

I also got a job at a new church that year after finishing seminary. I was now hearing sermons that took progressive interpretations of scripture and used them to call parishioners to direct political action. I was working in a building that housed several nonprofits: a refugee resettlement program, a nonprofit that supported formerly incarcerated persons reentering society, organizations that supported trafficking survivors and unaccompanied minors, and various other hands-on ways to practice what we preached.

For Christmas of 2021, one of my friends gave me Derecka Purnell's book *Becoming Abolitionists*. I finished that book ready to identify myself as a socialist—as someone who believes that society needs to be collectivized and systematized in such a way as to prioritize the needs and agency of all, especially those most historically exploited and marginalized. *Social*-ism as opposed to *capital*-ism; people, not profit.

In the second half of 2022, I read *Black Reconstruction* by W. E. B. Du Bois and the autobiography of Angela Davis. I emerged from those studies ready to identify myself as a communist—someone who believes in a world in which capitalism and class are abolished and industries are owned and administered by their workers.

And toward the end of 2022, I read a book called *Mutual Aid* by Dean Spade. It's a fantastic, short, accessible work; it is by far the best radical literature I've ever read.[3] He never actually says the word *anarchism* in it, but I was telling a friend about it, and she said, "Oh, yeah, I have a lot of anarchist friends, and mutual aid is sort of their whole thing." And I realized that the mutual aid groups that Spade describes, if scaled up to the level of an entire community and society, is essentially what anarchy is. I was so on board with Spade's ideas that I began to research anarchism, which led me to thinkers such as Noam Chomsky and Murray Bookchin.

At the end of 2022, I identified as an anarchist—someone who believes in the abolition of the state and all rulership. Now, you'll notice that anarchy is defined negatively by what it's against. However, as with socialism, communism, or most political philosophies, there are many schools of anarchism that each have their own positive articulations of what they are *for*. I'll explain what I am for in the next section, as well as more about what anarchism is.

For now, I'll end this chapter by emphasizing that the major turning points in my journey pivot more on people than on ideas. What made me a progressive christian was being challenged by progressive christians whom I respected and loved. What made me a leftist was meeting leftists I respected and loved. What changed

---

3. *Nonviolent Communication* by Marshall Rosenberg is a close second. Marshall Rosenberg, *Nonviolent Communication: A Language of Life* (Encinitas, CA: Puddle Dancer Press, 2015).

my view toward socialism and communism was coming to associate them less with totalitarian regimes and more with W. E. B. Du Bois, Cedric Robinson, and Angela Davis. What made me an anarchist was becoming best friends with someone who knew and admired a lot of anarchists.

I hope this book is written in such a way that allows you, the reader, to encounter an anarchist worldview from someone you can access and respect. The way I see it, that's how we grow.

Two

panoramic dreaming
what is anarchism?

Let's go back to seventh-grade english class and hit those greek stems. If patriarchy is rule by men, and monarchy rule by an individual, and oligarchy rule by a small group, then we can deduce that *arch* denotes rulership. Therefore, anarchy (*an-archy*) is non-rulership. Anarchy is a political philosophy that rejects rulers and rulership. At its essential, atomic, etymological level, it is no more, no less.

my flavor of anarchism

This is what all anarchists, all anarchies, and all anarchisms necessarily have in common. Within this, there are naturally many variations, many schools, many subtraditions. I am a Black pacificist utopian municipalist anarchist—say that three times fast. That is to say, in my visions of abolition, the revolution, and post-state reality, I have the following qualities. First, I am rooted in Blackness as, among other things, a condition of ontological ungovernability and anti-state orientation.[1] Second, I reject violence as a revolutionary tactic, as the means of revolution must always cohere with the ends (peace). Third, I fiercely believe in the limitless availability and accessibility of the good. Lastly, I anticipate a world in which communities associate freely in the form of communes or confederated municipalities— more on that shortly.

As someone who constructs his vision of an anarchist society within a postindustrial context, my philosophical system is not primarily built on the thought of first-generation european anarchists from the nineteenth century (e.g., Pierre-Joseph Proudhon, Mikhail Bakunin, or Peter Kropotkin) but rather on the thought of latter anarchists Lucy Parsons, Murray Bookchin, Lorenzo Kom'boa Ervin, William C. Anderson, and Marquis Bey.

As much as I appreciate Murray Bookchin, as a Black man, I look to Black anarchists for a crucial perspective that the former's social location—as a white dude from Vermont by way of New York— precludes him from offering. But since many Black anarchists, including Ervin and Anderson, either allow the use of violence or even expressly call for it,[2] I look to anarchist christians[3] such as Leo Tolstoy and

---

1. William C. Anderson puts this masterfully in his book *The Nation on No Map*: "Blackness has been relegated outside the state and the social contract . . . Blackness is anarchic, and Black people have been engaged in anarchistic resistances since our very arrival in the Americas . . . why not embrace the statelessness we're in, the statelessness we are, and organize through it and with it?" William C. Anderson, *The Nation on No Map: Black Anarchism and Abolition* (Chico, CA: AK Press, 2021).
2. Importantly, Dr. Marquis Bey does not: "When we are faced with imminent violence we must refuse to proliferate violence, because we've come into being via a violation and this bestows upon us the ethical commitment to mitigate that violence." Marquis Bey, *Anarcho-Blackness: Notes toward a Black Anarchism* (Chico, CA: AK Press, 2020), 17.
3. It's very important to me to say *anarchist christians* and not *christian anarchists*. The latter seems to imply that there is a kind of anarchism that is christian,

Vernard Eller to construct an utter rejection of violence out of Jesus's life and teachings. And yet many anarchist christians historically have been demystifiers™—folks who reject the supernatural and attempt to construct religious systems entirely devoid of it—as well as theocratic thinkers whose only offer of an alternative to the state seems to be the church, as if the only way to have an ethical society is for everyone to be christian. So ultimately I have to do what all anarchists must do—I must take all that I can, all that is liberative from each school of anarchism that I've studied and use it to construct my own understanding.

other aspects of anarchism

Philosophical gatekeeping and cults of personality are antithetical to the essence of anarchism. To say that there is some "authentic" anarchism or that one must be a Proudhonite or Bakuninite, etc., to be a real anarchist is to place one person in ultimate authority over all anarchists, which is of course the exact opposite of what anarchism teaches. All anarchists must believe in the abolition of the state because that is what the word literally means, and without that it becomes meaningless. But beyond that there is no expression of anarchism that is inherently more authentic than another.

Anarchism judges thought based on its own merit. One of the most important premises of anarchism is that we are all capable. All capable of leading, all capable of decision-making, all capable of administration, all capable of liberative thought and action. We don't professionalize any of these tasks; we democratize (anarchize) them.

---

which I reject, mainly because I see christianity as *being* anarchic much more than *qualifying* anarchism. It is much better to say there is a kind of christianity that is anarchist because even though that *should* be implied, it sadly is not—most expressions of christianity are indeed far from this.

Accordingly, there's no professional credential or guild that ensures "quality control" of anarchist thought, but rather it's the "peer review" of the entire movement that builds the strength of, and consensus around, our political philosophies.

Christianity is actually quite similar in this regard. There is no one tradition or expression of christianity that is inherently authentic in contrast to others. And yet in order for any such tradition to be an expression *of christianity*, in my view, it must include the tenet of Jesus as the Son of God. That is the most atomic definition of the word *christianity*, and without that, the word becomes meaningless.[4] But beyond this, christianity can, does, and should express itself in infinite forms.

And naturally, just as I do believe that utopian pacifist municipalist anarchism is one of the soundest and most liberative schools thereof, I also believe that anarchist christianity is the soundest and most liberative tradition thereof. But it would be a fool's errand to seek to promote that belief through gatekeeping. Rather, I seek to promote it by demonstrating its beauty, logic, and potency as best as I can and letting others engage with it freely in conversation with their own experiences, wisdom, and social location.

---

4. "But can't someone who follows Jesus's teachings be a christian even if they don't believe he was the Son of God?" That person can certainly do that and very likely construct an ethical life, quite possibly much more ethical than the lives of many who call themselves christians yet in fact follow some statist distortion of christianity. But what that person is doing, great and sufficient and beautiful though it may be, would not be properly termed *christianity*. Jesus himself claimed to be the Son of God. How can one be, and why would one want to be, a christian without taking Christ on his own terms? Unlike anarchism, christianity as a religion does, in fact, hinge unavoidably on one concrete, historical person, although it importantly does not in its dimension as a political and social movement—revolutions do not require, and in fact do better without central leaders, hence Jesus's literal removal of himself from the picture via the ascension.

One important aspect of anarchism is that it does not promote *chaos*. Anarchy does not refer to a free-for-all with no organization, no structure, or no administration of public life. It is truly a semantic bummer™ that the word is used popularly to mean chaos—just type "anarchy Elmo" into Google, and you'll see what I mean—because although the word *anarchy* is defined negatively, the political philosophy that bears its name is a robust, positive construction.

the politic and the philosophy

Anarchy[5] is a politic, a system of structures for the exercise and administration of civic power, in which public life is administered by the people, not by rulers—people who exercise power "on behalf" of others and thereby disallow the latter from exercising their own power; this includes "representatives." Anarchism is the philosophy, the system of ideas, that undergirds this political structure. These ideas include the following:

- People, when placed within societies and cultures that are built on principles of mutual care and dignity of all, will act cooperatively.
- Within such a society, therefore, people do not need rulers to coerce them to act in a certain way.
- Therefore, there is no justification for any person or group to have more political power than others; humans can simply administer their collective life through horizontal systems of free, voluntary association, and consensus-based cooperation.

---

5.   From here on out, I'm going to use *anarchy/anarchism* as shorthand for my own Black pacifist utopian muncipalist anarchy/anarchism.

- The state is, by definition, a system of professionalized rulership and coercion and is therefore both unethical and unnecessary within an anarchist worldview.
- Effective public administration can only happen at a scale where people can work together, *face to face*, to reach decisions, by consensus, that are in the best interest of all.
- This scale is the municipality. Any larger scale necessarily takes the form of a professionalized, bureaucratic state, which at its best operates representatively but nevertheless always tends toward dominion.
- Locally operated projects work better because our needs are best met by those with the most local knowledge. We are the ones best suited to make the decisions that affect us.[6] Imagine that!
- The state always tends toward dominion because representatives who, at best, intend to speak for a community can never do so as well as the community can for itself.
- People should be able to live in a society where they can develop their capacities freely, decide for themselves what their needs are, participate in stewarding the community's resources, participate in the collective decision-making process, and consent to the conditions under which they live.
- Governance and innovation should be local, while knowledge, support, and solidarity should be networked.[7]
- Municipalities should come together in free associations to coordinate their cooperative actions. These associations are often called *confederations*, *leagues*, or *communes*.

---

6. Dean Spade, *Mutual Aid: Building Solidarity during This Crisis (and the Next)* (Brooklyn, NY: Verso, 2020), 40.
7. Spade, *Mutual Aid*, 41.

- The ideological basis for such a society is not any one religion, spirituality, or philosophy but rather a universalistic
  ethic of love, cooperation, and care articulated through a
  free covenant into which citizens enter voluntarily. All spiri-
  tualties and philosophies that are represented in this plural-
  istic community both inform and are informed by this ethic.

These principles, expressed negatively as the demand for the abolition of the state, comprise the school of anarchism that can be
expressed positively as municipal libertarianism or ecological communalism.[8]

As you may have gathered, anarchy can also be thought of
simply as ethical democracy, if democracy is taken in its actual literal
sense of the people governing themselves (*demo-cracy*). Sadly, the
word *democracy* is another semantic bummer because it is used to
describe societies that are quite precisely the exact opposite of what
democracy actually is. Case in point: the United States of America,
which is *at best* a republic and in reality an oligarchy.

municipal libertarianism

Now, if you're anything like me, you hear the word *libertarian*, and
you immediately picture Ron Swanson at best and at worst the most
annoying dudes on Reddit. As with the popular usage of *anarchy*
versus its political meaning, this is—you guessed it, another semantic
bummer. Right-wing "libertarianism" is, at its heart, a belief in capitalism so all-consuming that it is unrestrained even by the government.

---

8. Murray Bookchin is the thinker primarily associated with this school of
    thought. Look him up on Google Images. He's such a cutie pie! So huggable.
    How can that cardigan contain such brilliance?

Everything in society operates according to the laws of competition, accumulation, and individualism without any intervention or regulation by the state. This is, of course, a recipe for complete antihuman disaster and the exact opposite of what classical libertarians believe in and work for. The fact that these two groups both believe in the abolition of the state makes them no more similar than democratic socialists and neoliberals who both believe in a strong centralized state. It's one overlapping means pursued for diametrically opposed ends.

So that's what municipal libertarianism is not.[9] But what is it? As the terms suggest, it is a political philosophy in which cities (municipalities) become the arena in which human beings, individually and collectively, can know true freedom (liberty).

what is a city?

How do anarchists understand the city? Geographically, we understand the city as the entity that includes an urban nucleus *and* its rural surroundings, which is how cities were traditionally understood from ancient times all the way up until the emergence of the modern nation-state.[10] This definition, of course, applies to towns and all kinds of municipalities as well. Politically and socially, the city is a human-scaled collective that comes together not through bonds of kinship or nationality but rather through bonds of shared ethics and proximity. Ideally, these ethics include equity, freedom—which we will define below—dignity, agency, inclusion, care for each other and

---

9. I'm not going to use the term *libertarian* much at all throughout the remainder of this book because it's not important to me to reclaim it from the Ron Swansons of the world. *Anarchist* is way cooler anyway.

10. Murray Bookchin, *From Urbanization to Cities: The Politics of Democratic Municipalism* (Chico, CA: AK Press, 2021), 273.

for the ecosystem, cooperation, and creativity. It is a community of voluntary associations governed by a people's assembly, which makes decisions through discussion and by consensus.

It's important to distinguish the ideal city, the anarchist city, from the urban megalopolis that exists in many forms today. Today, urbanization, which is generated by statecraft—the making and maintenance of states—and corporate capitalism, turns urban areas into vast homogenous and anonymous expanses. This is the exact opposite of what Bookchin calls "citification"—the process of creating cities, which by definition fosters diversity and deep connection.

Have you ever visited a new city or town, left the airport or train station, and watched as the landscape reveals the exact same endless series of aesthetically tragic strip malls, commercial highways, and nondescript housing developments that you just left behind in the place you traveled from? That's urbanization. Gentrifying developers forcing the mom-and-pop pizza shop out and putting a Starbucks in its place? That's urbanization.

But it doesn't have to be this way! As Sixtine van Outryve d'Ydewalle puts it, "Cities do not need to be ever-growing gigantic impersonal agglomerations dominating nature and ruling us . . . they can be, and in fact used to be, a place for the exercise of direct democracy . . . a place for us to meet, debate, and decide what we want to do collectively, rather than leaving this task to the professional politicians."[11]

Neighborhood folks coming together to shut down a new luxury apartment project and turning the space into affordable housing instead? That's anarchy, baby! Replacing shelter networks with mutual aid housing groups that squat on and develop unused or abandoned

---

11. Bookchin, *From Urbanization*, xv.

housing? That's anarchy. Childcare cooperatives, local power grids, and restorative justice centers? That's anarchy!

Anarchy brings the economy out of a private sphere, as in capitalism, or a separate sphere, as in authoritarian socialism, and into the public sphere. Economic policy, like all policy, is crafted by the entire community in face-to-face relationships working toward the common good. This turns the economy into an aspect of public affairs, which means it cannot become the self-serving enterprise that it is under capitalism and even under communism as state control of the economy inevitably tends toward its working for the state itself rather than for the people.[12]

In an anarchist city, the material means of life, the things we need and the tech and tools we use to produce them—goods, services, spaces, institutions, etc.—are controlled and distributed communally. Let's take housing as an example. People need places to live, so there's a local housing organization that handles the construction and maintenance of housing. That local organization is funded by the community, administered by the community, and accountable to the community. As each city freely cooperates with other cities in the form of confederal networks, which we'll discuss shortly, each housing organization cooperates with other cities' housing organizations, and in this way resources and best practices are shared to prevent redundancy.

Everything that people need not only to live but also to develop their capacities fully is organized and administered on this principle. In this way, everyone contributes according to their ability, which itself is fostered and cultivated by the community's communalist way of life, and everyone receives according to their needs.

---

12. Bookchin, *From Urbanization*, 273.

what is freedom?

If anarchism is a political philosophy in which cities become the arena for freedom, what is freedom? Old-school anarchist Mikhail Bakunin puts it this way:

> I am a fanatic lover of liberty . . . not the purely formal liberty conceded, measured out, and regulated by the State, an eternal lie which in reality represents nothing more than the privilege of some founded on the slavery of the rest; not the individualistic, egoistic, shabby, and fictitious liberty extolled by . . . the schools of bourgeois liberalism . . . no, I mean the only kind of liberty that is worthy of the name, liberty that consists in the full development of all of the material, intellectual, and moral powers that are latent in each person; liberty that recognizes no restrictions other than those determined by the laws of our own individual nature.[13]

Freedom is the ever-present opportunity to develop individual and collective agency and capacity to their fullest. Anarchists believe that individual freedom is channeled and expanded by an ethic of communal care.

what happens beyond the city?

As we've alluded to, anarchism does not envision a world full of parochial cities that exist as islands unto themselves, operating entirely apart from anything or anyone outside of them. The belief that governance must have its root in the city does not imply that the world can function as a collection of closed municipalities.

---

13. Noam Chomsky, *On Anarchism* (New York: New Press, 2013), 8.

Instead, anarchism calls for free association among cities. This cooperation operates by the same ethics that govern cooperation at the city level: care, dignity, and respect. These associations have historically been called *confederacies*,[14] *leagues*, or *communes*. How is this not simply the state by another name, you ask? One of the key differences is that these networks are entered into voluntarily and can be left voluntarily. This is not true of a state—not the modern nation-state and certainly not the traditional empire. Second, whatever political substance and authority communes derive from the cities that comprise them. As opposed to the state, which seeks to subsume municipalities under its umbrella (i.e., "you, city, are now part of the Roman Empire, you are now part of the United Kingdom, you are part of the German Democratic Republic, you are a creature of the U.S. federal government"),[15] the commune has no identity or substance apart from the cities that comprise it. Most cities today derive their political reality from states, whereas confederacies derive their political substance from cities. Third, leagues of cities do not govern so much as they coordinate the self-governance of cities in such a way as to make them the most collaborative, most positive-sum, and most effective. They have no power within themselves to coerce any municipality to do anything, but rather they have the function of coordinating municipalities' doing of that which they have already consented to do of their own free will.

---

14. This is another semantic bummer if you're from the United States, but, again, having one okay structural idea means nothing without an ethic of love, which obviously the Confederate States of America did not have. Also, the Confederacy was not a libertarian league of cities so much as a loose alliance of fiefdoms. It was decentralized not for the sake of democracy but rather for the sake of each plantation's maintaining its own autonomy as a parochial kingdom, and that was why it had no need for centralized authority.
15. This is how the US Constitution describes cities within its territory.

Confederal or communal councils are composed of delegates endowed with imperative and recallable mandates by their popular assemblies. That is to say, their agency is not a static substance that resides in their professional position but rather a dynamic that flows from the people—namely, their commissioning of delegates for specific tasks and their ongoing consent to be represented thus—to the delegates. And as such they can be recalled at any time. These delegates are not political professionals but rather nonprofessional spokespersons conveying the decisions of their assemblies to the confederal council.[16]

Here are some examples of things communes can do:

- Organize and maintain networks for distribution of resources and products
- Deal with regional concerns such as coastal erosion, lanternfly invasions—those beautiful locusts—and large-scale transportation
- Plan and execute large-scale research projects (e.g., exploring the deep seas, curing cancer, putting a human on Mars)
- Many of the things, like the above, that we currently look to a coercive, bureaucratic, ineffective state apparatus to do

a dialectic of interdependence and autonomy

Another important thing to say about the commune is that municipalities that participate in communes exist within what can be called a *dialectic of interdependence and autonomy*. We'll get more into what a dialectic is in the next chapter, but for now we can say that it's a dynamic where two seemingly contradictory things are not only both

---

16. Bookchin, *From Urbanization*, xvii.

true but actually true *because of* each other. In this case, the municipality that is part of the commune has to be both dependent on
other municipalities within its commune *and* truly self-sufficient and
autonomous. "How can this be?" you ask. It all comes down to solidarity, which is true of most tenets of anarchism. People who truly
believe in and live according to the principle of solidarity (*philia* in
greek, which is cool because we often translate that word as "love")
can do both—they can take full and ultimate responsibility for their
own needs and their own collective life (autonomy), *and* they can
recognize the need for and the beauty of cooperation among different municipalities (interdependence). How lovely this is!

We can be healthfully autonomous only when we recognize that
the principle of solidarity on the municipal level quite obviously has
to extend beyond that to all people, and we can be healthfully inter-
dependent only when we recognize the full agency, capacity, responsibility, and sufficiency of each individual municipality. This works on
the next lower level of complexity as well: individual persons are certainly better in community, and yet communities rely for their health
on the full freedom, agency, and self-definition of their individual
persons.

an atomic model for the commune

Please allow me to pull from my stunningly far-ranging mastery of
chemistry to offer an analogy for how communes work.[17] In a confederal model, municipalities are like atoms, and communes are

---

17. I failed organic chemistry in college, actually. Took one look at that final exam
     and walked down the thirty stairs of that lecture hall, plopped my booklet
     down, and proceeded right out the door. Did fine in gen chem though. *Sun-
     glasses appear on me; Biggie's *Hypnotize* plays in the background.*

like molecules. Individual atoms bond to form molecules. And the people who represent the community as confederal delegates are like electrons. Electrons don't act on their own, but they do interact with the electrons of other atoms to make connections and work cooperatively.

Do electrons "rule" the nucleus? Certainly not. If anything, the nucleus has the power. But the electrons still play a very important purpose in shaping the kinds of interactions the nucleus can have with other nuclei, and as such the electrons are a big part of what gives the atom its unique character. Electrons have very important functions, but they certainly do not rule the nucleus or have power over the nucleus. What gives the atom its essential character—its atomic number—is its nucleus. The electrons, for their part, determine how the atom interacts with other atoms, which is very important, but their agency very clearly derives from that of the nucleus.

The neutrons and protons are the people, the nucleus is the people's assembly, the electrons are the delegates, and the molecule is the commune.

And molecules can take infinite forms! They can be made up of two atoms or two thousand. They can be made up of all the same element or many different elements. They can take on a variety of different molecular structures. They can react with other molecules. So with communes. They can be made of two municipalities or five. They can have constituent members who are relatively similar or relatively diverse. They can take on whatever function and working structure that they find best. They can be an organization of municipalities or of regional bodies or even of continental bodies.

This is how anarchism envisions intercommunal relations, and the cool thing is this has very much been done throughout history. These kinds of decentralized, voluntary confederal associations of cities were a feature of the medieval period, for one. We're talking about the Lombard Leagues in Italy, the Swiss Confederation, the Hanseatic League of central and northern Europe, the Rhenish Leagues of Germany, and more.

historical examples approaching municipal libertarianism

On that note, here are some of the most prominent and/or successful examples of anarchic principles at work in world history:

- The democracy era of Athens (ca. fifth century BCE)
- The Gray Leagues (Graubünden) of Switzerland from the sixteenth century to the turn of the nineteenth century
- The *comuneros* of sixteenth-century Spain
- The American town meeting movement of the 1770s
- The sectional citizens' assemblies of 1790s Paris
- The Madrid citizens' movement of the 1960s and '70s

Each of these movements represented part of the anarchist vision I've laid out here and also fell short of it in significant ways. Some of them had dynamic people's assemblies but did not include all people. Some were inclusive but made critical errors in the areas of gradualism and compromise with the state. There is no one shining moment in history that we can look to and adopt wholesale, but there is an *immense* amount of historical support for the principles and practices of anarchism.

are anarchists against authority?

Anarchists reject authority in the forms of hierarchy, domination, coercion, and even representation. We reject any political arrangement in which any one individual's agency is taken away, nullified, or vested in another person. Anarchy is a situation where everyone has agency and everyone exercises their agency to *support* others in a way that helps them to develop their own agency and personhood. It is not power *over* (rulership) but power *for* (care). No one is governing anyone, no one is above or below anyone else, but everyone is tasked with the work of fostering, collecting, and amplifying the voice of every individual within the collective.

Those who have civic power have it, by definition, for the purpose of doing a specific job that they've been asked to do and that needs to get done (e.g., keeping a meeting on track, representing the perspectives of one's community). It's not the role that justifies the actions (i.e., I can do such and such because I'm the leader); it's the actions that justify the role (i.e., only if and when I am doing my job the way I've been asked to, the way folks have consented to, do I have this power at all). When power is exercised in this way, hierarchy is both unnecessary and unhelpful.

is this not a pipe dream?

"Okay, Terry, this all sounds really lovely in a theoretical, kumbaya sense, but we live in the real world, and I really don't see how to get from this world to the one you're describing."

Immanuel Kant said, "Freedom is the precondition for acquiring the maturity for freedom, not a gift to be granted when such maturity is achieved."[18] In other words, the good news is that we don't have to wait until the world, or our country, or our city, is "ready" for anarchy. We don't have to wait for an ideal moment when the stars align, when the variables come together in the test tube, when the

---

18. Chomsky, *On Anarchism*, 8.

climate is right. Rather, the more we start to live according to the ethics of anarchy (cooperation, communalism, etc.) now—that is, the more we exercise the freedom we currently have in accordance with the best ethics—the more ground we will gain for freedom.

This happens at the most micro and the most macro levels. We can undergo personal revolutions within ourselves, including abolishing the "cops" in our heads that tell us to live by certain scripts and tell us to judge other people for not doing so. We can root out rulership and homogenizing norms in our interpersonal relationships, in our families, in our civic organizations, and so on.

As we do so, the means have to cohere with the ends. Statism can never be a "transitional tool" to get us to liberation. We cannot teach ourselves how to live in a free world through coercion. There will certainly be a transition—complete anarchy will not be achieved overnight—but that transition will occur through ever-widening circles and practices of anarchy, not through (seeking to) wield the tools of the state to force an anarchist takeover, an oxymoronic intention, which is why authoritarian socialism is also an oxymoron.[19]

The more we get active in mutual aid groups, which are mini-anarchies, the more we will make anarchism a reality. The more we create alternative institutions that replace and obsolesce those of the state (e.g., conflict mediation centers to replace police, grassroots housing organizations to replace the US Department of Housing and Urban Development, health care cooperatives and clinics to replace our morally bankrupt and logistically depraved health care system, etc.), the more we will make anarchism a reality.

---

19. Also known as *Marxism*. "Communism" does not have to be authoritarian, but historically it usually has been, and when it has not been, it's been better described as anarchism. Even democratic socialism is just a diet form of authoritarianism. State bureaucrats, whether appointed or "elected," are always corrupted by the inherently harmful nature of rulership itself.

Lorenzo Kom'boa Ervin calls for neighborhoods and communities to build *dual power*, that is, to function as liberated zones outside of and counter to the control of the government. He sees the *commune* as a center of social revolutionary culture, an actual alternative to the state and the primary organ of the new society. Ervin, William C. Anderson, and many other Black anarchists point out that not only is the commune certainly something we can begin building now but also something that Black people *have* constantly been building throughout the histories and afterlives of slavery, colonialism, and capitalism. Black folk, and other oppressed peoples, have always built survival programs to meet the needs that the state has shown itself unwilling and/or unable to meet. We have built our own mutual aid projects, our own housing and food cooperatives, our own community safety structures, and our own systems of self-governance. Black anarchism offers the crucial insight that for Black folk, the state has always been obsolete, and the commune has always been possible and often real. The sooner we can realize these truths, and therefore reject reformist, liberal, and even "progressive" desires to make the state include us and serve us—which it cannot do and will never do—we will see just how imminently practical and reachable the commune is and always has been.

It's important to remember that for much of human history, life has been organized around and rooted in the village, town, or city. Yes, states emerged early, but they existed in a parasitic relationship to cities. They did not replace cities as the hub of communal life; rather, they drained the riches of those cities—resources produced precisely by their communalism. It was not really until the emergence of the modern nation-state that the ruling class was able to successfully alienate people away from an identity rooted in their neighborhoods and municipalities and instead homogenize them into an amorphous national identity.

So the question is not really whether or not human society is best organized at the level of the city. History makes it abundantly clear that it is. The question, rather, is whether or not human society can be successfully and sustainably *reorganized* this way today in our bloated statist world. Proponents of centralized societies would say no—municipalism is a pipe dream that doesn't work because humans are naturally self-centered, greedy, and individualistic; the state is the only way to account for and manage—that is, police— these tendencies. And also modern human society is super complex and can only be administered by an equally complex, professional bureaucracy.[20]

Anarchists reject this worldview as a thinly veiled retroactive philosophical justification for the economic and political views that the ruling class, and those they successfully co-opt, already hold— namely, that it is meet and right for a small group of people to hold exponentially and increasingly more power and resources than the vast majority of people.

Anarchism is certainly utopian. Anarchism is about rejecting all of the depraved and bankrupt messaging that tells us we can't have a just and functional world. It's about setting our face fully toward lib- eration. But anarchism is not a pipe dream. It is quite the opposite—it is the most practical way for society to be organized and quite pos- sibly the only way for society to be organized such that we evade the complete self-annihilation that is fast approaching as a world built on domination and rulership collapses under the weight of its own inter- nal contradictions. Murray Bookchin puts it this way in *Post-Scarcity*

---

20. But this is a circular argument. Society is incomprehensibly complex precisely because of the statism and urban sprawl advanced by corporate capitalism. Take that away and—voilà—society can once again become human-scaled and comprehensible.

Anarchism: "No longer are we faced with Marx's famous choice of socialism or barbarism; we are confronted with the more drastic alternatives of anarchism or annihilation. The problems of necessity and survival have become congruent with the problems of freedom and life. They cease to require any theoretical mediation, 'transitional stages' or centralized organizations to bridge the gap between the existing and the possible . . . the possible, in fact, is all that can exist."[21]

conclusion

Anarchism is "a new politics structured around towns, neighborhoods, cities, and citizens' assemblies, freely confederated into local, regional, and ultimately continental networks."[22] Power is decentralized and popular rather than centralized and bureaucratic. The city is the locus of human life because it is the only human-scaled political arena where people can work face to face in order to govern themselves by consensus. It is for this reason that the city is the only arena where "humans can reach their full potential in reason, freedom, and creativity through discourse and collective decision-making."[23]

---

21. Murray Bookchin, *Post-Scarcity Anarchism*, 3rd ed. (The Anarchist Library, 1986) (Chico, CA: AK Press, 2004), 35.
22. Murray Bookchin, "Municipalization: Community Ownership of the Economy," *Green Perspectives*, no. 2 (February 1986), https://libcom.org/article/municipalization-community-ownership-economy.
23. Bookchin, *From Urbanization*, xviii.

Part Two: An Anarchist Theological System

Now that we've briefly outlined what anarchism is, we get to my favorite part—using anarchism as an organizing principle for a systematic theology. That is to say, we get to see how the building blocks of christian faith comprise one of the many spiritualities that add flesh and color to anarchist philosophy, and we get to see how anarchism in turn clarifies and illuminates the tenets of christian faith. Let's get into it!

Three

God is a lover, not a ruler
anarchy in the Trinity

authority in God

A lot of anarchists are atheists precisely because they equate the idea of God with the idea of coercive rulership. And understandably so—the Bible often seems to present God that way, and surely the history of christendom has presented God that way.

You guessed it—I don't see God as a ruler. "How so," you ask? I'm so glad you asked.

First, let me start by restating that this book is a systematic theology, which means that it constructs a system of theological beliefs that are primarily organized *logically* rather than *narratively,* as they are in the Bible. As you may have noticed, each chapter of part II of this book covers a different concept or category of concepts having to do with religion (e.g., God, humanity, revelation). The progression is conceptual rather than chronological or textual.

Systematic theologies use logic and the humanities (history, literary studies, comparative studies, sociology, psychology, etc.) to construct understandings of spirituality that are rationally, historically, and ethically sound.[1] So, on one hand, a biblical theology might look at, say, the biblical idea of divinely ordered genocide or divinely facilitated conquest and exile of the Jewish community and from this conclude that God is a coercive and/or violent ruler. But, on the other hand, an anarchist systematic theologian would use logic and literary studies, among other disciplines, to clarify how even those texts that become scripture may not—and, I'll argue in chapter 5, *cannot*—historically *always* be an accurate or a reliable depiction of the will or mind of God.[2] An anarchist reads sacred texts knowing they contain the voice of rulers *and* the voice of the ruled, and as such, as well as for many other reasons, must be viewed and filtered through the lens of virtue and logic, in conversation with the Holy Spirit.

Such a reader would recognize that when scripture depicts God as exercising their[3] authority violently and coercively, that is the voice of rulers and/or the voice of a colonized mind. That reader would also recognize that when scripture, much more generally and broadly, I would argue, depicts God as exercising their authority through *care*, this is the voice of virtue and logic coming through.

In chapter 5, we'll come back to the question of how to know when and why to question or reject certain scriptural ideas and

---

1. Please note that I'm not saying here that spirituality can be "rational" in the sense of "totally explained or circumscribed by reason." Spirituality can be characterized by rationality, but it by definition cannot fully be accounted for by reason alone. Spirituality deals with the nature of being(s), while rationality deals with the nature of concepts. So spiritual beliefs should hopefully be informed by reason and not be anti-rational as are, say, patriarchal theologies, but they (e.g., the question of whether God can become incarnate) cannot be elucidated solely by reason.
2. Sounds like I don't believe in inspiration, doesn't it? I actually do. Peep chapter 5.
3. I will be using they/them pronouns for God as God is nonbinary, which is both self-evidently true and something that Janelle Monáe tweeted once.

motifs and the theological basis for doing such a thing. For now, let's take a look at the scriptural thread of God as a caring supporter and contrast it with the thread of God as a coercive, violent ruler.

Genesis

Genesis chapter two. In this allegory God creates human beings, and then does God rule them? Certainly not. God does not coerce them to do anything but rather gives them agency and power to do what God could have done themself (e.g., name the animals). God cultivates their capacity by shepherding[4] them through their two fulfilling and delightful tasks of tending to the garden and tending to their relationship. They care for each other, for animals, and for the earth.

Oftentimes a helpful way to interpret scripture is with scripture. We can use the second creation account in Genesis 2 to help us interpret the first account when the latter reports God as saying, "Let us make humankind in our image, according to our likeness; and let them *rule* over . . . all the wild animals of the earth." The way humans interact with creatures and the earth in Genesis 2 demonstrates to us what the word *rule* means in Genesis 1. It's not the authority to coerce or dominate. It's the *responsibility* to care. *And if this is how humans are to "rule," and if they are made in God's image, then this is also how God "rules."*

---

4.   Genesis 3 tells us that after Adam and Eve eat the fruit of the tree of the knowledge of good and evil, they "hear the sound of God walking in the garden in the cool of the day." This implies that they know what God's tread sounds like. They recognize the sound because it's something that has happened regularly. In this allegory, God walks with humanity daily and carries on a relationship with them.

Now, I'm not arguing that the communities that produced the text of Genesis 1 didn't have a view of rulership or dominion characterized by coercion and domination. They very likely did, as almost every ancient near eastern society did. What I'm arguing is the remarkability of the fact that *in spite of that*, there is nevertheless a strong thread of noncoercive power associated with God throughout scripture, starting in the first book of the canon.

Now, from Genesis 2 onward, God certainly often tells human beings what they want them to do. God tells Adam and Eve that they can eat from every tree except one. God tells Noah to make an ark. God tells Abram to pick up and leave his ancestral homeland. God tells Moses to liberate their people. God gives the people the mosaic covenant and instructs them to follow it.

But, first of all, is that God commanding them to do something under threat of coercion? Or is it better understood as God asking, inviting, or appealing to them to do those things?

Second, and this will help us lean a certain way on the first question, what does God do when we don't do what they ask us to do? Do they force us to do those things anyway? Do they violently punish us for not doing them? Many people would say yes to both of those questions, right? Scripture seems to say yes as well. But an anarchist christian would apply a particular theological lens to these motifs of divine coercion and punishment in scripture—a hermeneutic[5] of care, one might call it—and use this lens to faithfully understand these motifs in light of a basic theological commitment that God is good.

---

5. A hermeneutic is an interpretive lens or filter. Just as everyone sees the world through particular, unique eyes, everyone employs a particular scriptural hermeneutic based on their social location, theological commitments, experiences, and so on.

an anarchist reading of Genesis 3

We can begin with Genesis 3, the allegory that paradigmatically poses and answers the above questions—particularly, how does God respond when we don't do what they ask us to do?

> The LORD God said to the serpent,
> "I will put enmity between you and the woman,
>   and between your offspring and hers;
> he will strike your head,
>   and you will strike his heel."
> To the woman he said,
> "I will greatly increase your pangs in childbearing;
>   in pain you shall bring forth children,
> yet your desire shall be for your husband,
>   and he shall rule over you."
> And to the man he said,
> "Because you have listened to the voice of your wife,
>   and have eaten of the tree
> about which I commanded you,
>   'You shall not eat of it,'
> cursed is the ground because of you;
>   in toil you shall eat of it all the days of your life;
> thorns and thistles it shall bring forth for you;
>   and you shall eat the plants of the field.
> By the sweat of your face
>   you shall eat bread
> until you return to the ground,
>   for out of it you were taken;
> you are dust,
>   and to dust you shall return."

Now, understanding that this is an allegory, and furthermore noting that the formatting of this part of the story shifts from that of prose to that of poetry, the reader versed in literary studies will understand the rhetorical nature of the literary devices employed here:

- Common human phenomena are referred to as *curses*. This is a rhetorical device that crystallizes, foregrounds, and sharpens the effect of the former in the story.
- These "curses" are attributed to direct divine decree, which is also attributable to the simplifying nature of allegory. Allegories usually don't deal with complex ideas like indirect causation—that would defeat the purpose of allegory, which is a narrative genre that seeks to portray common motifs in very simple terms, often terms that a young child can grasp.

In light of all of this, an anarchist would employ their understanding of rhetorical device, ancient near eastern worldview, and basic theological truths to interpret this story as a parable that allegorizes various universal human realities by portraying them in a(n) (over) simplified form, parabolically attributing to divine "curse" that which in everyday experience is better attributed to natural consequences of societal patterns and structures. Such a hermeneutic delivers a radically different interpretation than the traditional reading:

- Humans, in seeking to meet their genuine needs for provision and security, are regularly faced with a choice between solidarity and supremacy. The latter choice is the paradigmatic stimulus of human harm, symbolized in the story via the forbidden fruit.
- Humans' choice to seek to rule rather than care for each other (Adam turning on Eve, blaming her for his choice,

etc.) leads to humans' choice to seek to rule rather than care for the earth. Rejecting animal husbandry in favor of animal domination. Rejecting the fruits of the earth's natural bio-diversity in favor of bio-domination through monocultural production of agricultural commodities, deforestation, and climate violence.

- The serpent, in addition to representing animals, alternatively represents Satan. The "curse" (the natural consequences) of rulership in all its forms—oligarchy, patriarchy, heterarchy, white supremacy, etc.—comes to us when we buy into the logic and methods of rulership, which Satan personifies. When we allow rulership, rulers will strike our heads from above, while we at best will strike their heels from below. But as long as we follow the logic of rulership—as long as the "curse" persists—we will never defeat rulership itself; we will never cut off the head of the snake.

- Painful childbirth? You can't tell me that without the stultifying effects of rulership, we wouldn't have innovated a way for people to give birth entirely without pain. We've created many technologies, medicines, and procedures that already go a long way toward this, and we've done this within depraved health care systems that exist to make a profit and not to care for people. Imagine what we could've done by now if we rejected the forbidden fruits of profit and accumulation.

- "Your husband will rule over you"—is patriarchy a fate that God places on humankind as punishment for sin? Or is it allegorized in this story precisely because it is universally one of the many natural outcomes of adopting a rulership worldview?

- Painful toil required to produce one's daily bread? A futile or often adversarial relationship with the earth? These are also

the consequences of rulership. Anarchy fosters the cooperation and creativity needed to remove toil from human
work—without rulers we would innovate and cooperate
unwanted work out of human society in no time at all. And
without rulership our relationship with the earth itself would
be one of care and symbiosis. The thorns and thistles of eco-
cide and climate disaster would be a shameful thing of the
past.

- You will surely die? The story itself makes clear that this
refers not to instantaneous physical death but rather to
spiritual death—the death of the spirit, which character-
izes the existence of many under capitalism and statecraft.
The spiritual death whereby individuals adopt the logic and
methods of rulers. If we refuse the forbidden fruit of self-
supremacy, we live—we remain free to construct societies
that make life abundant for all.

Let me say a quick word on the forbidden fruit. In the story, it comes
from the "tree of the knowledge of good and evil," right? Many
interpreters have taken this to mean that God wanted Adam and
Eve to stay in a state of naive innocence forever, having no concept
of right and wrong. Knowing what evil is is tantamount to doing or
being evil.

I disagree with that. The hebrew word often translated into english as *know* is often not best understood as meaning simple awareness or comprehension. The word for *know* is often used in the
Hebrew scriptures to mean "had sex with," you may remember.[6] The
word often refers not to simple awareness but rather deep engagement, profound experience, or intimate relationship. So I don't think

---

6.   "And Adam knew his wife Eve" (Gen. 4:1).

the thrust of Genesis 2–3 is that human beings were never supposed to know what evil was. It's that we were not meant to become intimately engaged with it. We were not meant to enter into or become one with it. We were not meant to become familiar with love only to then choose supremacy. We were not meant to believe that we could have it both ways. We were not meant to value supremacy equally or even greater than solidarity, believing that evil (rulership) can provide us something helpful (abundance) that in reality only good (cooperation) can.

So the allegory is not wistfully harking back to some time of widespread ethical naivete. Humans have always known what good is—we were created in the image of a good God: "Ever since the creation of the world God's eternal power and divine nature, invisible though they are, have been understood and seen through the things he has made."[7] As soon as Eve rolled up on the scene, Adam understood how to treat her ethically, as "bone of his bones and flesh of his flesh"—as part of him. He knew that to be alone—whether literally or figuratively, through not treating this other person as his equal and his beloved—was bad.

The other tree in the middle of the garden was the tree of life. What kind of tree would contrast with a tree of life? A tree of death. "Knowledge of good and evil" is just a subtler, more poetic way to say *death*. It might better be translated as the tree of "intimacy with good and evil," again, in the sense that we have decided to cheat on solidarity with supremacy. No good tree bears bad fruit, nor does a bad tree bear good fruit.[8] Each tree is known by its own fruit. Indeed, figs are not gathered from thornbushes, nor grapes from brambles.[9] If the

---

7. Romans 1:20.
8. Luke 6:43.
9. Luke 6:44.

fruit is described as causing instant death—"when you eat of it you will certainly die"[10]—then the tree is quite certainly a tree of death.

So in the middle of the garden, Adam and Eve have a crystal-clear set of two options: life and death. The choice is free. It is not coerced by God or anyone else. Rulers and their conscious and unconscious supporters would love for us to think the choice between the two is complex, just as the serpent tried to portray it to Adam and Eve. But it's not. Not for these allegorical characters and not for the people they represent (us).

We've always had a clear choice between life and death. The book of Deuteronomy tells us as much: "See, I set before you today life and prosperity, death and destruction."[11] Genesis 3 allegorizes the choice we all have before us—a choice that is clear and free. The story allegorizes the way that death presents itself as life, as fruit that is aesthetically and gastronomically pleasing, even when life itself is all around for us to see and have our fill of. The forbidden fruit is self-supremacy, which is synonymous with death. The choice has always been clear, and yet because it has always been a free choice, there's always been the possibility of humans choosing death even as it's so clearly the wrong choice.

And here's the key with respect to God: *God does not intervene by preventing us from choosing it, or punishing us when we do choose it, but rather by making appeal after appeal and demonstration after demonstration that we might choose of our own accord to turn around. And God makes the ultimate appeal in the person and movement of Jesus Christ.*

The "curses" of Genesis 3 are allegorical representations of the universal consequences of the ways in which humans have chosen

---

10. Genesis 2:17.
11. Deuteronomy 30:15.

to act and construct their societies around the value of supremacy, repeatedly rejecting God's appeals to us to exercise our own agency in service of care. As allegories are designed to do, this particular parable naturally oversimplifies the theological dynamic of God's interaction with and response to human choices by casting it all in terms of direct divine rulership, reflecting an ancient near eastern worldview. Yet history demonstrates clearly that in everyday experience, *the situation we have is not a divine punishment but rather the direct consequence of our own choices. God "allows" these outcomes because God is not a coercive ruler who forces their will on the world but rather a lover who, while seeking to foster our growth, will not use coercion or violence to determine our conduct.*

divine authority and the problem of evil

Ethics cannot be forced. Ethical maturity cannot be externally determined. It is, by definition, something one *chooses* to do. Why doesn't God force the world to be good? Because that's not a logical possibility any more than the idea of God making a triangular square. So the age-old objection of "If God exists and/or is good, how can there be evil or harm in the world?" is a logically fallacious question. Created beings cannot develop ethically except by their own free choice. If it is forced or determined, it's not virtue.

However, even if we throw out the illogical question of "why doesn't God force the world to be perfectly good?" we still have another question about God's authority. Why doesn't God exercise their authority by intervening against at least the most egregious forms of harm? Why didn't God prevent the Shoah or American chattel slavery?

God does intervene. It's just not in the way we expect. *It's not in the form of coercion or domination. It's in the form of appeal, in word and action.* But because we equate authority with coercion, we completely overlook God's intervention—it doesn't fit within our philosophy of power.

When we step away from allegories—useful as they are if handled responsibly—when we enjoy the benefit of hindsight and look at God's action throughout history, when we hold our theologies and worldviews up to the refining fires of experience and logic, we come to see quite definitively that God does not coerce or dominate. If God were a coercive ruler, God would have simply prevented all instances of harm, not least the most mammoth systemic structures thereof. But, of course, this would defeat the purpose of creating humans in the first place as we were created in the image of God, which necessarily includes agency and freedom. So God does not intervene in the sense of coercively preventing either particular human actions or the systemic accumulation of human actions.

Nevertheless God certainly *does* intervene. God intervenes by exercising their authority in the way they always do—through care. God does not prevent humans from choosing self-supremacy, but they intervene by telling us in clear terms what the natural consequences of that choice will be, in hopes that we *repent*, in hopes that we turn around and walk the other way, in which case those things will not come to pass. God intervenes by showing up and persuasively demonstrating a better way. God does this through the theological appeal and politically persuasive witness of prophets who clarify, afresh for every generation, the choice that the people have between life and death. God does this through providing a covenant full of ethical principles that, if observed, guarantee life. God intervenes by providing other ethical teachings through sages. And most notably, God intervenes by becoming a human person who makes the way of life and love as abundantly clear and as fully extended as existentially possible. And then the Holy Spirit continues to do this until we enter

God's complete presence—complete in extent and in degree—in the eschaton.

Why didn't God intervene against X, Y, or Z? God did! God came closer to us than we thought was possible and gave us the clearest, most persuasive demonstration possible of how to prevent and eradicate X, Y, and Z. But *we* have to do it! God is not going to do it for us or over or against us—God made *us* more than capable of doing it! And how do we do it? By giving absolutely zero quarter to the philosophy or practice of rulership, refusing to cooperate with it even if that noncooperation leads to our physical death. Obsolescing the state and embracing anarchy even if that leads to our execution by the state at the behest of the people. This is why Jesus says,

> The hour has come for the Son of Man to be glorified. Very truly, I tell you, unless a grain of wheat falls into the earth and dies, it remains just a single grain; but if it dies, it bears much fruit. Those who love their life lose it, and those who hate their life in this world will keep it for eternal life. Whoever serves me must follow me, and where I am, there will my servant be also. Whoever serves me, the Father will honor.[12]

If my this-worldly life is more important to me than love, my priorities are out of order. If staying alive is more important to me than the movement, I've lost sight of what the movement is about. The movement is bigger than any one individual. It's about the people. And it may come to be that the best way to care for the people is to give up my own this-worldly life to continue to undermine and obsolesce the logic, methods, and essence of the state.

If that is true of me, and I hope it is, there are many people who will interpret that as my hating my life. Not valuing my life enough.

12. John 12:23–26.

And yes—in comparison to how much I love *love*, how much I love the movement, how much I love the people—you could say that my feelings toward my own this-worldly life register so far below this that they register as "hate."

Now, the truly remarkable thing would be if I felt and acted that way without any sense of what happens after death, if anything. The message of Good, which in this context means *holy*, Friday is that even before resurrection is something feasible or something we have sight of, to die rather than betray love is a holy act.

But thankfully I *can* think back to all the times when Jesus told me he was going to be killed *and* raised to new life. Thankfully, I can think back to when Jesus actually followed through on that. And I can know that there is a next-worldly life that can never be distorted by rulership and will never end.

This is what Jesus demonstrated to us. This is how God made their appeal to us. This is how God intervened against harm—by giving us the exact playbook on how to not only defeat it occasionally but also to eradicate it permanently. It's up to us! Rulership ends if and when rulers have no one to rule. Jesus showed us how to become ungovernable! Moses showed the Israelites the choice between life and death by giving them a covenant by which they could make rulership obsolete and make life abundant. Jesus showed the world the choice between life and death by giving us a renewed covenant—the Sermon on the Mount—by which we can make rulership obsolete and life abundant. It doesn't depend on what rulers do. It's up to us.

In all of this, please don't hear me as victim blaming. I'm not saying that oppressed peoples are ultimately responsible for their own oppression or that they could end their oppression simply by acting ethically or anarchically. What I'm saying is more that rulers are not omnipotent. We don't have to resign ourselves to oppression as long as there are people with the will and power to oppress. Becoming ungovernable will most likely involve suffering (i.e., carrying our crosses, losing our lives). The movement is not in itself the end of suffering; it is the path to the abolition of exploitation. We can't control what people do to us, but we can always control the path we walk. And walking the path of liberation will likely not itself end our suffering, but it will always undermine the cause of our suffering, and *it will eventually lead to freedom*. The storms will come, but the house built on the rock will stand.

how does God's authority work?

I don't have the space in this book to respond to every instance of apparent divine coercion and violence in scripture, but let me summarize my anarchist hermeneutic in this way: our theology, namely our understanding of who God is and how God works, acts as a filter for all of the many communications by which God speaks to us (we'll discuss this further in chapter 5). Therefore, if we believe that God is a coercive, violent ruler or if we associate all authority with coercion and violence, as many people in the ancient Near East understandably did, we will naturally hear God saying, for example, "X will be the consequence of Y action or Z inaction" as "I will do X to you if you do Y or fail to do Z." We'll automatically hear, "I'm asking you to do X" as "I'm making you do X, under threat of force." We'll hear, "Go to location X and live ethically"[13] as "Go to location X and commit genocide against the people there because you are better than them."

---

13. Anarchists don't believe in nations or borders, so an anarchist would not interpret this first directive as imperialistic. The land belongs to the people collectively, and there's more than enough for everyone to live off of if they live ethically. No borders, no limits on mobility or migration, just hospitality and cooperation.

What about the texts that claim to be reporting immediate, direct, supernatural punishments from God—opening up the earth to swallow Korah and company, for example?[14] As I see it, an anarchist hermeneutic can either completely reject any historicity in these texts or it can surmise that something dramatic did happen, just not in the exact way or through the exact causation that the text reports. Sinkholes are real, right? The possibility that Korah fell into one of those and that tradition interpreted it as an act of God feels unlikely but a lot more likely—to me—than the idea that a good God supernaturally punishes people Wile E. Coyote style. Bears do occasionally maul people, right? Would they ever do so on prophetic command (2 Kings 2:23–35)? Probably not, but it sure makes for an interesting story, and I'm sure it somehow served the purposes of the people who recorded it and passed it down.

In all, our worldview heavily influences how we receive and interpret what God is saying to us. Along the path by which scripture arrived to us today, it passed through many voices and pens of people deeply influenced by a statist, deterministic, punitive, and/or violent worldview. This is not new information. There is a consistent but not singular thread throughout history of people and communities choosing to live by such values.

The good news is that our theology is not a closed system that can't receive input from the outside. God lets us freely construct our worldviews and, of course, also recognizes that we *receive* a worldview from our communities, many components of which remain hard for us to penetrate rationally or volitionally, but God also constantly appeals to us with their own "worldview," demonstrating their ways to us. This often results in changes to our worldview, whereby we deconstruct harmful or regressive views of God and adopt healthier ones. One

---

14. Numbers 16.

of the many metanarratives of scripture is this very progression—nonlinear and frustratingly slow as it may be at times—from less accurate or virtuous theologies to more accurate and virtuous ones.

Nevertheless, this progression, when it does happen, happens in steps, not leaps. So don't hear me as speaking ill of my ancestors in faith who espoused views that I am now rejecting. I'm grateful for the work they did in understanding God, and I'm doing exactly what they would want me to do—building on it. Taking the wheat and leaving the chaff. But no one can harvest wheat out of chaff if someone hasn't first planted and cultivated the crop. I hope my descendants in faith will find some value in the planting and cultivating I did. I know I sure do with regard to the planting of my ancestors.

The point of this chapter so far has been to demonstrate how reading scripture in conversation with sound insights from history, literary studies, cultural studies, and ethics provides an interpretive lens through which to read it in a way that reveals reliable theological insights about God. The Bible is one very important tool through which we study and come to understand how God's agency works, among other theological questions, but it can only be utilized healthfully if we look at it with lenses that clarify, rather than distort, the concepts on which it touches.

If we do this, we will see that God exercises their power not through coercion or domination but rather through care. God fosters our development of our ability. God invites us to confer with them on how they should exercise their power. God invites us to participate in their exercise of their power. How incredible is that? God stewards our abilities to do these things by guiding us as individuals, guiding us as communities, listening to our concerns via prayer, allowing us even to impact God's own course of action through our petitions and our sharing of our hearts with them. Remember the time Abraham negotiated with God? Remember the time Moses led

God to "change their mind"?[15] Remember the time God became a human so that no part of the depth of human experience would be left unplumbed or unincorporated into divine experience and solidarity? This is the type of power of which we speak when we call them *Almighty God*. Get hype! Where are my organ interjections at?

reclaiming and subverting God-talk

On that note—as with many outdated and regressive terms, those of us who are convinced that God is not a ruler are free to either subvert or reject rulership language around God. That is to say, we can reclaim terms such as *king, lord, kingdom of God,* and even *rule* itself, or we can replace them with terms such as *lover, healer,* or *kin-dom.*

By the way, y'all have to understand that I'm from a state whose motto is "Virginia is for lovers." I always mean the word in an expansive, evolved way that's inclusive of all kinds of love. Liz Lemon might get bummed out by any use of "lover" not between the words "meat" and "pizza," but I sure don't.

Subverting traditional language around God might take the form of transforming our understanding of what kingship, lordship, and kingdoms can and should look like, both currently and eschatologically. I will be the first to say this is quite difficult to do. But this is the option I choose, not least so that I can still make use of all of my doxological resources (psalms, other sacred texts, Darlene Zschech bangers, etc.) that use such language. Part of that for me looks like recognizing my own semantic history. With the way my life has gone, the word *lord* doesn't really call to mind knights and dukes; it's almost exclusively associated with Jesus for me. And the word *king* makes me think less of traditional kings—I just don't have any

---

15. Genesis 18 and Exodus 32, respectively.

firsthand experience with those—and more of memes about short kings and the youthfully colloquial way of calling everyone *king* or *queen,* although I prefer the gender-neutral "yes, chef." Doesn't mean I'm not susceptible to regressive applications of these terms to God—I certainly am—but it just helps me on my path to subverting and reclaiming them.

God is not a ruler, Adam and Eve were not rulers, and neither are we

As the Gospel of John points out about five hundred times, Jesus and the Father are one. Trinitarian theology would say the same—each person in the Trinity acts in tandem. They have the same intentions, the same will, the same methods. If Jesus walks and talks the politic of care, so does each person of the Trinity. If Jesus rejects coercion and domination, so do the Parent and the Spirit.

So, of course, if this is the way God governs the world, how much more should we seek to eliminate all forms of dominion and instead govern ourselves the way Jesus taught us? And isn't our imitation of God's own intra-trinitarian, horizontal, anarchic self-care a foretaste of the day when we will enter fully into that very communion, as we were first created to do?

Everyone has agency, and we are meant to exercise that agency through *care.* The greatest among us is the greatest caretaker. God lives this way, and so should we.

freedom in God

Not only do I believe that God has power and exercises that power through care, but I also believe that God exercises their power *freely.* God is a free agent—not in the NBA sense but in the more general sense that God is free to exercise their agency however they choose, although of course the NBA meaning[16] is derivative of this—and this is one of the "communicable attributes" that God imparted to human beings when they created us (along with creativity, sociality, etc.). This means that anything God does, they do because they *choose* to, not because they *have* to. In the same way that human history is not deterministic in the sense that humans *had* to do the things we've done by virtue of some controlling law of the universe that we cannot violate, neither is cosmic history deterministic in the sense that God *had* to do the things they have done.

Why is this important? Because, as we've alluded to, freedom is prerequisite to love. Love is only love if it is chosen freely. If it is automatic, if it is predetermined such that it could not possibly be anything else, if it is coerced, it is something other than love. The sense in which God *is* love is precisely this dynamic in which the Persons of the Trinity *choose*, unfailingly, to relate to one another through and in love. Theologians call this ongoing, unbroken dynamic of intra-trinitarian love *perichoresis*. Freedom is the foundation and the prerequisite for the love through which and by which all existence has meaning, purpose, and delight.

Now, in the same way that human freedom is constrained and channeled by human nature (e.g., I am not free to fly because my nature is such that I cannot fly), there are certainly ways in which divine freedom is channeled by divine nature. Is it *possible* for God to not love? No because God, by nature, *is* love. The action of love and the nature of love are eternally present in a timeless God.

Here's a tougher question: Was it *possible* for God to not redeem humanity? Oof. It could definitely be argued that extravagant,

---

16. Spurs nation, lift up your heads! Yea, even though we have walked through the valley, we have been called once again to stand on the summit!

boundless care is intrinsic to God's nature such that to not redeem humanity would have violated God's selfhood. Now, does this make the fact that God *did* redeem humanity less significant or wondrous or unmerited? Of course not. The fact that God *is* love does not at all take away from the beauty of the fact that God chooses, invariably, *to* love, and neither does it take anything away from the beauty of God's particular choice to love in the form of redemption.

Here's a question I think is more open-ended: Was it *possible* for God to not create the world? I feel pretty positive saying yes. As much as I like to think of the creation of the world as the inexorable over-flow of God's intra-trinitarian love spilling out of the Godhead and into other repositories and generators of love (i.e., creatures and especially human beings), I don't think that God's nature *demanded* that they do that. In fact, it might be a theological fallacy to say that the existence of God *has* to lead to the existence of non-God creatures. God, by definition, is self-sufficient and an end in Godself and cannot necessarily imply or require the existence of other beings in order to properly be God.[17]

So it was divine freedom, in the form of love, that led to the voluntary creation of all nondivine things. And the fact that the world is made of the *stuff* of free, noncoercive, trinitarian love is so, so beautiful and so significant. It means that this is how our world—logically, intrinsically, properly—must properly *operate* as well.

---

17. I had a neo-reformed professor in seminary who was so committed to his system of christian determinism that he insisted that anything God has done, God *had* to do, and also God, in some sense, has *never not* done because God is immutably deterministic or deterministically immutable. This led to him using a whole bunch of grandiloquent language to do an impressive amount of theological gymnastics in order to prove that God has *always* been incarnate, and God has never *not* been Creator, etc. As you can imagine, I recoiled against this but at the time didn't quite have the language for why/how I disagreed.

a dialectic God

One more thing about divine freedom. Freedom implies the ability to change, does it not? The freedom to act in a new way, to move in a new direction, to become something that one was not previously? Yet we say that God is unchanging, do we not? Immutable, if you're fancy. Are we at an impasse? Is this where logic breaks down or finds its limit?

I don't think so. We might just need a higher form of logic. This is where dialectics comes in. Now, I'll be honest with you—this is a word that I heard *all* throughout seminary, and yet when I got my diploma in the mail (thanks, COVID-19), I still did not have the slightest inkling what it meant. It was only when I started to listen to a podcast in which a precious British dude[18] explained Marxism that I had my Michael Scott "why don't you explain it to me like I'm five?" moment.

A dialectic can be understood as a situation where two seemingly contradictory things are not only true at once, which alone would just be a paradox, but actually true precisely because of the other. *Dialectic* can be a noun referring to such a situation or an adjective referring to such a condition. Perhaps the best example to use is the dialectic of change and continuity. A tree is a thing, a stable object, but it's also a moment along a continuum from a seed in the ground to carbon in the ground. It is both, and each aspect depends on the other. I am the same person I was ten years ago—Terry Stokes, grandson of Burnie, player of Spikeball and guitars—but I'm also a completely different person than I was ten years ago. I cannot be who I am without both of those things being true, and neither can be true without the other. Far from being a contradiction that leads to

18. John Molyneux, *Introduction to Marx/Marxism*, podcast audio.

breakdown, this is a dialectic that ensures my synthesis, my constitution as a dynamic, living being.

As the precious British podcaster guy puts it, "Any existing thing is . . . a moment of balance or equilibrium between opposed and contradictory forces—forces that make for change and forces that preserve the status quo."[19]

A dialectic nature is one of the communicable attributes that God gave to us. In fact, it can be argued that to be a being is by definition to have such a nature. And just as we are unities of change and continuity, so is God. God is not a static metaphysical[20] entity but rather a being and the very embodiment of this interchange of change and continuity. So the idea that God is immutable is true but incomplete and false if taken as complete, just as "Terry is the same guy he was ten years ago" is true but incomplete and false if taken as complete. God, as a being, is both change and continuity. For us to say that God is the same yesterday, today, and forever is 100 percent true in a very concrete, evident way, *and yet* it is also 100 percent true to say that God, especially as Love, is constantly expanding, subsuming, and deepening. The way that God "changes" is kind of an "infinity + 1, infinity + 2" situation or a "further up, further in" situation as in Aslan's country.[21]

---

19. John Molyneux, "Dialectics," *Introduction to Marx/Marxism*, October 2020, podcast audio.
20. This is another one of those words that I pretended to understand but really didn't. Metaphysics is the realm of ideas. Are ideas "things"? Are they "real"? Plato, an "idealist," would say yes; Marx, a "materialist," would say no. This is one of the questions that the discipline of metaphysics seeks to answer. So here I'm just saying that God is not merely an idea or a concept.
21. If you're unfamiliar with this reference, you're in for a real treat. I hate to say it, but you should stop reading this right now and go read *The Last Battle* by

Why is this important? I'm sure there are other ways to accomplish this, but for me, this resolves the tension between God as immutable and God as dynamic. Scripture is very clear that God is constant, and this is a huge source of comfort and stability for many christians, including me. However, scripture is also very clear that God *acts*, and on a very basic level, to act is to change, is it not? God, in order to interact with the world, must do so in a dynamic way; otherwise, there can be no real connection, no real access point between God and humanity. Scripture reports that God changes their mind on occasion.[22] God allows freely contrived human thoughts and intentions to influence God's actions. God became a human person. God incorporated humanity into Godself. How can that be understood except as some form of change within God?

In other words, the idea that God is dialectic is important because it allows us to move out of an impasse between seemingly contradictory truths about God's nature and reach a higher, fuller, synthesized, more complete understanding of God that recognizes that change and continuity are only contradictory in a physical sense, not in a metaphysical sense.

We'll return to the idea of dialectics in chapter 5 when we talk about how God communicates with humans.

conclusion

God is a triune community whose persons relate to one another through an ethic of love—that is, care, affection, recognition, respect, commitment, trust, and communication. This is how bell

---

Clive Staples "C. S." Lewis, or DJ Clive, as I call him. I'm part of the Clive Hive. I shop at Staples.

22. Exodus 32:14; 2 Samuel 24:16; Jeremiah 26:19; Amos 7:3; Jonah 3:10.

hooks defines *love*. She also calls it "the will to extend one's self for the purpose of nurturing one's own or another's spiritual growth."[23] I think these are two beautiful ways of understanding and delineating that virtue for which and through which all things exist. In all communities, including the Trinity, this ethic of love requires freedom, exists dialectically, and operates through collective, egalitarian care and cooperation. These are the principles of anarchy at work within the life of God. This is what power originally looked like. Accumulative individuals and groups appropriated the concept of power, making it synonymous with domination and coercion. But God, while allowing themself to be misunderstood and misrepresented, has never *actually* acted in the ways these people have claimed God does. In God's actions, they have always gone to lengths to reclaim the concept of power as care, most definitively in the person of Jesus Christ.

---

23. bell hooks, *All about Love: New Visions* (New York: HarperCollins, 2001), 4.

Four

the people are alright
anarchy in humanity

Let's talk about the concept of human nature. I mentioned earlier that supporters of centralized authority (e.g., liberals, most
conservatives, authoritarian socialists, democratic socialists, etc.) say
that anarchism is a pipe dream that doesn't work because humans are
naturally self-centered, greedy, and individualistic, and the state is
the only way to account for and manage—that is, police—these tendencies. I also said that anarchists reject this worldview and instead
assert that people, when placed within societies and cultures that
are built on principles of mutual care and dignity of all, will act cooperatively and caringly, and in such a society we do not need rulers to
coerce us to act a certain way. Here is where I give my theological
defense for this anthropological viewpoint.

traditional understandings of sin and salvation

You may be familiar with the doctrines of *original sin* and *total depravity*.
Without getting into the weeds on these, suffice it to say that taken
together, these doctrines teach and/or imply the following ideas:

- Genesis 3 tells a historical account of what christians later termed *the fall*, a discrete moment in time when the first two human beings rebelled against God, which caused "sin" to enter not only the world but also human nature.
- This sinful nature was then passed down hereditarily to all subsequently born humans.
- Thus, before any individual person is born, they are both permeated by sin (sinful, sin-full) and guilty of sin. Their *origin* is sinful (original sin).
- Sin very quickly permeated the full extent of both individual human nature and collective human existence (i.e., society, culture).
- The redemption accomplished by Jesus Christ saves persons (by grace, through faith) individually from the consequences of our sins (justification) and gives us a new nature (regeneration) whereby we are actually capable of choosing the good and being made holy (sanctification). However, this does not counteract or end the hereditary propagation of humankind's sinful nature. Each human being continues to be born with a sinful nature.
- Those human beings who are redeemed experience a tension between their sinful nature and their regenerated nature (i.e., the old and the new self, the flesh and the spirit), the latter of which is not passed down metaphysically in the same way that the former is.
- The eschatological[1] return of Christ will eradicate sin once and for all, such that those who enter into eternal life will no longer have a sinful nature nor experience a sinful society.

---

1. An eschatology is a belief about the end times.

I lived the majority of my life believing each one of these points wholesale. No notes. But as my faith was slowly radicalized, cracks turned to fissures, and eventually the whole structure needed to be replaced with something else.

harm

Many traditional christian understandings of the world hinge on the concept of sin, as the above illustrates. Based on my christian experience, I recently realized that I have framed sin primarily as a transgression of some cosmic law of rightness and wrongness, which would make God the cosmic law-giver (legislator), law-interpreter (judge), and law-enforcer (cop). It would also require that the solution to the problem of sin be some metaphysical overwrite—legal pardon—as opposed to a free, voluntary, life-giving repair accomplished cooperatively by living beings.

I've been wondering if this is a helpful and enriching way to think of human actions. I've had some recent experiences in which my framework for sin turned out to be severely inadequate for understanding and responding to what happened. I also read an incredible book called *Nonviolent Communication*[2] that significantly helped me to consider and adopt a different framework.

In light of all this, I've come to think in terms of *harm* rather than *sin*. I try to use an empathic framework for harm rather than a legal one. I try to think of harm in terms of unmet needs rather than in terms of transgression of cosmic laws and metaphysical categories of right and wrong. I was taught to think in terms of spiritual indictments, judgments, and verdicts, but now I try to think in terms

---

2.   By Dr. Marshall Rosenberg, please read this!

of observations, statements of feelings and needs, and requests for reparative measures. I was taught to think in terms of punishment, pardon, and commuted sentences—reduced from eternal torture and incarceration to smaller sanctions—but now I try to think in terms of moving compassionately through grief, regret, and contrition into empathy, awareness, emotional intelligence, and virtue. I try to think in terms of liberation from and repair of harm, as opposed to salvation from a *condition* of wrongness or a consequence of punishment.

The idea that we exist in a cosmic "state" with universal laws, judges, courts, cops, and prisons has been around as long as there have been rulers who've wanted to construct theologies that reify and justify their own rulership systems. It took me a while to realize that this is perhaps the state that most needs to be abolished.

An important part of abolishing the state is abolishing the "states" in our heads. There's a little cop in my head who wants to police people. There's a little judge in my head who wants to judge people as right or wrong. There's a little lawbook in my head that wants to present its legal code as more eternal, fundamental, and valuable than humanity itself. What I can do to obsolesce all three of them simultaneously is to learn to approach harm through a person-based framework that allows me to connect with the feelings and needs behind my actions, as well as with those of others.

This is generative and open-ended. No policing, no judgment, no appeal to metaphysics. If I harm someone, I'm able to keep my focus on them rather than on laws and concepts. I don't get weighed down by guilt, shame, or fear. Instead I think about the real feelings that I neglected to acknowledge and the real needs that I was trying to meet through what I did. I can think about a more life-enriching way to acknowledge those feelings and go about meeting those needs in the future. I can think about the feelings of the person I harmed and how their needs were obstructed by what I did.

The way to repair harm that hurts someone's feelings and neglects their needs is to work toward acknowledging those feelings and meeting those needs. This may be a process we get to participate in, if it's okay with the person we harmed, or it might be a process handled by their support system and the community more broadly.[3]

Jesus has made a way for us to repair and prevent harm by acknowledging people's feelings and needs, in a way that helps us to build personal habits that help us to grow ethically—out of empathy and solidarity rather than guilt or shame—as well as to build relationships and communal practices that help us, individually and collectively, to heal from hurt and to become beloved communities.

Am I recommending that we all stop using the word *sin* or a sin framework? Not necessarily. Everyone interprets spiritual concepts in light of their own experiences, commitments, and desires. There are as many understandings of sin as there are people. Does yours genuinely serve your growth in love? If so, cool.

But if you're like me and it maybe does not, and therefore needs to be jettisoned, that's also fine. Was humankind made for the Sabbath or the Sabbath made for us? Were we created and retrofitted to some fixed eternal framework of sin, or was it—at best—developed to help us to love?

What I do know is that rulers love it when we think in terms of right and wrong instead of solidarity and supremacy. It's much easier to control the definition and application of concepts than to control people's understanding and honoring of spiritual realities. Rulers love it when we use right and wrong as middlemen for feelings and needs, or perhaps more often as smoke screens for feelings and needs. Their

---

3. We look at an example of this in practice in chapter ten, where you'll notice that restorative justice doesn't need to appeal to any metaphysical concepts of sin, right, or wrong, nor to legal categories or systems. It focuses on the feelings and needs of people and communities.

goal is to get us out of touch with our feelings and needs because as soon as we are in touch with them, as soon as we reconnect with the empathy that is at the root of our humanity—that is when we rise up and throw off structures, systems, language, and concepts that do not acknowledge our feelings and do not meet our needs.

break it down and build it back up

If you're like me, moving away from a legal framework for harm and toward an empathic one is an *Extreme Makeover: Home Edition*, or at least one of the lighter renovations that Bobby does on *Queer Eye*. But if you're like me, you're not new to this. We've de- and reconstructed before. It's hard but it's rewarding as heck. So let's revisit the foundation. Starting with our origin stories.

I would interpret Genesis 2–3 as an origin myth,[4] like many others from its era, that crafts a stunning allegory in order to say true things about humanity. Humans were created by God—however directly or indirectly, immediately or gradually—and participated in the life of God through love and cooperation, but humans then chose instead to reject solidarity in favor of supremacy. That is, they chose to seek to meet their needs for autonomy, freedom, and security by making themselves rulers rather than cooperating with others. This led to choices that harmed their relationships with others and with God. Most attempts to respond to these instances of harm, if not centered on feelings and needs, can and have led to more harmful choices rather than repair. The accumulation of these dynamics into a way of life creates more and more alienation, scarcity, and unfulfillment.

---

4.   Or an origin legend, if Adam & Eve were real people who were mythologized like John Henry was.

an anarchist anthropology[5]

An anarchist christian might therefore view humanity as follows: As creatures of God, who is good, human beings necessarily have a fundamentally good nature—not in the sense of immediate ethical perfection, which for creatures takes time and development, but rather in the sense of creaturely beauty and ethical orientation. Goodness is a communicable attribute of God.[6] How can we be made in the image of God and not be built for care, solidarity, and love?

Yet as those who bear the image of God we also have agency, and sometimes we use our freedom to try to meet our needs in ways that end up being harmful to us and/or to others, whether intentionally or unintentionally. The most enriching way to repair this harm is to empathically connect with our genuine feelings and needs, as well as those of others, and work together to find ways to acknowledge and meet them in a way that enriches life for everyone. If we are unwilling or unequipped to connect with feelings and needs, we are likely to continue the cycle of harm. We continue the cycle of harm through legal frameworks, believing that an appeal to some cosmic law will standardize perceptions of and responses to harm. We continue the cycle of harm through authoritarian frameworks, believing that giving someone a monopoly on coercion and violence can resolve or at least manage harm by force.

Early human history contains plenty of examples of cooperative societies that predate noncooperative and/or statist societies. The latter way of living is by no means primary or inevitable for human civilization. Unfortunately, when would-be rulers come to think that they benefit from noncooperation, and when the ruled come to

---

5. In theology, an anthropology is a belief about humanity.
6. "God saw all that they had made, and it was very good" (Gen. 1:31).

think of harm repair primarily in legal or statist terms, most people become individually and collectively disconnected from the feelings-and-needs framework—the empathic framework they need in order to live cooperatively. Over time, enough communities became sufficiently alienated from empathy that rulership becomes dominant in the world.

But, thanks be to God, humans have always had the opportunity to start anew and build a collective life on the cooperation, care, freedom, creativity, etc. that God created us with. Many communities have taken that opportunity. But many of those communities have been unable or unwilling to implement a feelings-and-needs framework for harm repair that would sustain solidarity.

an anarchist soteriology[7]

Alright, we've redone the foundation; now we need to redo the ground floor. What does all of this mean for what we traditionally call salvation? How does Jesus save us if not from our sins?

In theology, answers to the question of how Jesus saves us are called atonement theories. Within a couple of centuries of Jesus's life, the early church had already developed several prominent atonement theories or *models*. Several of the more classic and well-known models can be thought of together under the heading of *substitution*. Jesus *took our place*. Jesus subbed in for us and took our punishment, our shame, our guilt, our consequences on himself, and we got to receive his perfection.

There were other atonement theories, too. The *christus victor* model taught that Jesus saved us by winning a cosmic victory over the

---

7.   A soteriology is a belief about salvation.

powers of supremacy and scarcity—vanquishing them. The *ontological healing* model taught that when God became human, this opened the door for humans to become divine. Jesus saves us through *theosis* or *divinization*.

One of the earliest atonement theories was the *moral influence* theory—the idea that Jesus saves us through influencing people to live ethically. Does this sound milquetoast to you? It certainly did to me when I first encountered it. Not cosmic enough, not spiritual enough, not comprehensive enough, not silver-bullet enough. Plus all of the best church bangers had substitution language in their hooks. The moral exemplar theory just didn't go hard enough.

Let me ask you this, though: Who stands to lose the most from the moral influence model? Is it not rulers whose rulership would quickly become obsolete if people truly began to live the way that Jesus taught us to? Rejecting violence and coercion like he taught in the Sermon on the Mount, rather than entrusting them to the state and then worshipping the state for the very violent coercive power we've given it? Rejecting authoritarianism like Jesus did during his temptation in the wilderness, rather than clinging to it to solve our problems? Choosing to die rather than allow ourselves to be co-opted by the state? Inviting people to freely enter into cooperatives rather than appealing to bureaucracies?

There may be a reason why the moral influence theory is not a prominent atonement model for many christian traditions. There are some powerful people who likely have been very motivated to make sure that it either receded or morphed into something a little less threatening.

But as I rebuild my theology, slowly and painstakingly, I'm less and less compelled by the idea of a top-down metaphysical rewrite of reality. I'm more compelled by the idea of a decentralized movement that organizes people to freely cooperate in transforming the world collectively. I'm less compelled by the idea of salvation from metaphysical conditions and more compelled by salvation from individual and collective habits and structures that cause and perpetuate harm. When I hear the words *born again*, I picture regeneration into a new life resurrected from alienation and scarcity, alive in solidarity and abundance. When I hear the word salvation, I praise God that I'm saved not from an inherent depravity but from the obstruction of the inherent divinity we were created with and for. You better believe I still cling to forgiveness, but forgiveness in a relational sense, not in a legal sense.

I absolutely believe in a cosmically victorious Jesus, and I very much believe in a Jesus who opens up the door to *theosis*, but I can't practically enjoy *christus victor* or *ontological healing* unless Jesus shows us a way to live that repairs and prevents harm. Thank God that Jesus did so by putting us in touch with our true feelings and needs.

He shows Zacchaeus that his need for security will be better met through solidarity with the people than through taxing them on behalf of Rome. And he acknowledges his feeling of self-loathing by picking him, him, out of a huge crowd of people and choosing to stay at his house. *Me, host the greatest rabbi of our time and quite possibly the Messiah? Clearly he sees something in me that I don't.*

He shows the woman at the well that her need for provision, which she has been looking to marriage to provide,[8] will be better met through the mutual aid of a whole community unified by a spirituality centered on spirit and truth. He acknowledges her feeling of

---

8.   Likely via the law of levirate marriage which in the case of the death of each of her husbands (sudden and widespread death was common) would have required one of their relatives to marry and provide for her.

rejection and hopelessness by choosing her to become an evangelist of hope.

He shows Peter that his need for safety and dignity would have been better sought not through denying him, but through being willing to be humiliated and even martyred on account of him. Jesus acknowledges Peter's feeling of shame by overwriting his threefold denial with a threefold confirmation of love and a prediction of his martyrdom. The harm has been repaired and Peter will get another chance at this.

He shows the woman about to be stoned that the way to repair whatever harm she's done will not be through punishment or condemnation, but through empathy and restoration. He acknowledges her feeling of isolation by interrupting his teaching to care for her.

Time would fail me to tell of all the times that Jesus approaches, prevents, or repairs harm through connecting people to their feelings and needs. But this is what he does. He creates and consummates a movement built on the principles that humans were originally created to pursue, as well as the principles by which many human societies have organized themselves—equity, solidarity, cooperation, and creativity. This, done on the individual level and on the communal level, is how Jesus goes about empowering the people to change their world.

what about the cross?

Jesus continues to do all of this even when it inevitably pisses off rulers whose position depends on people remaining out of touch with their needs and feelings and in touch with authoritarian responses to harm. He refuses to stop organizing in this way even when rulers respond by murdering him. Jesus did not *have* to die. Jesus accepted death when his bodily freedom and autonomy were stolen away and there was no longer any other way to remain true to who he was.

Here's something that I believe with all my heart: God never needs to use bad things to accomplish God's purposes. God is, of course, able to bring good out of bad things, as God ineffably did with the cross. But God, as a perfectly good and capable being, never *depends* on bad things happening for the accomplishment of their purposes. God does not need to use harm to repair harm—even if that did somehow make logical sense. God did not need people to reject, betray, humiliate, and execute Jesus in order to accomplish reparation and liberation for humankind.

God coming to earth, and our uniting to God in Jesus, would have been more than sufficient for our liberation. The incarnation of Christ and our faithful reception of the new world order of God, as embodied and ushered in by Jesus, would have solved the problems that needed to be fixed. Or, perhaps more aptly, this would have repaired the harm that had been done and demonstrated how to increasingly reduce harm in the future. Our adoption of Jesus's ethics would have been sufficient to overcome the internal and external consequences of the ethics we had adopted.

Moreover, Jesus was the human who fulfilled that for which humanity was created—that is, a human life that by its faithfulness and love leads to full participation in the life of God. Enjoying his care for us, and following his example by participating in him and his care for the world, would've accomplished the very purpose, the very *telos* of our existence.

So, what does the cross represent if not salvation from sins? How about the exposure of the moral, pragmatic, and spiritual bankruptcy of rulership? How about the demonstration of the power of ungovernability? How about the presentation of the superiority of self-giving, uncooptable solidarity?

Now, did Jesus need the cross to accomplish these things? Certainly not—he had already done it in his life and ministry. But beyond that, he was able to turn this horrible (but common) tool of roman terrorism into one of history's most enduring and powerful symbols of love. The cross was never necessary, but that which Jesus subverted it into was and is. And, of course, the empty tomb confirmed, consolidated, magnified, and extended that which Jesus accomplished on the cross.

conclusion

Jesus's moral influence, especially his demonstration of harm repair, serves as the ethical and spiritual scaffolding by which human beings can subsequently live cooperative lives and construct empathetic societies. This rebirth, this regeneration into a life of empathy is one of Jesus's many gifts to humankind. Just as God regenerates individuals, God regenerates human communities. At any given time, human societies are capable of receiving the gift of Jesus's movement and trusting in God's ways of cooperation and love. At any given time, human communities are capable of choosing to nurture love through a focus on feelings and needs. Therefore, a better world is never out of reach.

If we succeed in creating those new systems, yes, it will still be possible for humans to, at times, get out of touch with their own feelings and needs and/or those of others, and thereby harm each other. But we will be equipped to repair that harm, and the more that we do this, the more empathically developed we will become, which will reduce instances of harm in the future.

For all of the above reasons and others, anarchists reject the narratives with which the state constructs an essentialized anthropology that legitimizes its practices. We reject the mythology of charismatic leadership because—you guessed it—it teaches that we need to be ruled by people who know better than us. And we reject the doctrines of original sin and total depravity because statists created them in order to retroactively justify their own system of rulership by the allegedly self-evident idea that humans are naturally sinful and, lo and behold, the state is the best way to manage and police that sinfulness. The state presents itself as the only way for us to have protection from the rampant depravity and chaos that are ostensibly always implicit and explicit in human nature. We need a central bureaucracy of professional rulers, so it goes, to exercise a monopoly on violence to keep the worst impulses and expressions of human nature at bay. Now, obviously—*gestures around at everything*—this is nonsense. But many of us who recognize that haven't gone so far as to reject the view of human nature that undergirds it—I know I didn't for a good while.

Take a look at the most anarchic—most egalitarian, horizontal, and decentralized—societies around the world, both today and in history, and you'll see humans demonstrating . . . solidarity? Better, at least? Who could've predicted this? Take a look, for example, at how societies respond to natural disasters—by and large, they create ad hoc mutual aid structures, and they sacrifice time and resources to help one another out. This happens not least because disaster zones are effectively anarchist zones. The state either intentionally withdraws, or if it does engage, it responds ineffectively because it cannot and will not help in ways that challenge the very status quo that it exists to uphold. Consequently the people have to step in and—you guessed it—govern themselves.[9]

---

9. Spade, *Mutual Aid*, 46–47.

Anarchism, far from operating wishfully against human nature, is the political system that best accounts for what human nature actually is—cooperative. Statism is founded on an anthropology of greed and self-supremacy that then retroactively justifies its ethic of domination, competition, individualism, alienation, and scarcity. Anarchy is founded on an anthropology of care and love, which in turn makes possible an ethic of cooperation, communalism, and abundance.

Five

did I hear that right?
anarchy in revelation

Because anarchism has something to say about God and something to say about humanity, anarchism consequently has something to say about all forms of divine-human interaction, including God's act of expressing themself to humankind. This is called *revelation*.

revelation is a dynamic

"All Scripture is God-breathed and is useful for teaching, correction, rebuke, and training in righteousness" (2 Timothy 3:16). This verse is seared into my long-term memory. I probably got a badge for memorizing it in AWANA.[1] Some translations say "inspired by God," but I prefer the NIV because the greek is *theopnuestos*, literally "God-breathed." This is the only time this word appears in the

---

1.   This is how evangelical my childhood was: every week I went to a club where we got badges for reciting Bible verses from memory. Approved Workers Are Not Ashamed, boi! (2 Tim. 2:15).

Bible. It's likely that the author of this letter made it up for this very occasion.

Entire doctrines of inspiration and/or revelation have been built on the foundation of this one verse. Many thinkers have taken *God-breathed* to mean that scripture is inerrant—a term deeply qualified by what that person considers to count as an error—or infallible, or perfect, or perspicacious, which does not mean *sweaty*, as I initially thought but, rather, *clear*.

Here's the thing, though. You know what else is "God-breathed"? Human beings. Genesis 2 says that God formed Adam from the dust and breathed life into him.[2] Are humans inerrant, infallible, or perfect? No—we are created as good, beautiful beings who must exercise our agency, with God's help, to freely choose love and thereby enter further up and further into God's goodness.

"Okay, but scripture is not a being; it is a static entity created by God and gifted to humans, so therefore it can be inerrant," one might say. And I would then say, "The Word of God is *living and active*—sharper than any double-edged sword, it penetrates even to dividing soul and spirit, joints and marrow. It judges the thoughts and attitudes of the heart" (Heb. 4:12). The word of God is the speech act of God, the communication of God. The word is alive because *speech communication is a living, dynamic, two-way exchange*. Scripture is a record of God's past communication with their people, and God uses scripture today as part of a multifaceted way of communicating in a *live* way with us. The words on the page may be static,[3] but the process through which *the speech act of God for us in this*

---

2. And yes, this is an allegory, but it is poetically and theologically true in the same way that 2 Timothy 3:16 is.
3. And even these are contested, as demonstrated whenever you look up a verse and find twenty different translations.

moment arrives to us is dynamic, not least because speech communication always consists of both what is said *and* what is heard, which are not always the same. What we hear from the Holy Spirit, as we discussed earlier, is always affected and filtered by our experiences, our worldviews, our systems, and the overall nature of our relationship with God.

What constitutes the *word of God* is never about exact phrasing on a page. If that were the case, there would simply be no word of God to speak of at all—there's no book in the Bible that God dictated word for word and that has remained in that form ever since. The speech act itself was about the idea, not the exact wording. And then with every oral performance thereafter of that "word" or text, the wording changes, but hopefully the ideas remain in their essence—and they often do, but we should nevertheless use our discernment knowing that this doesn't always happen, and oftentimes rulers go to lengths to make sure it *does not*. Same with every act of copying, editing, redaction, and translation.

revelation as incarnation

Every year during Christmastide, I think about how wild the incarnation is. God became a human person! God cried! God got the munchies! God cuddled with their homies![4] God knows what it's like to think someone's waving at you when they're actually waving at the person behind you! That's wonderful! Get hype!

One thing I've always wondered about is how Jesus's humanity and divinity interact and cooperate in different situations. Does Jesus have omniscience in some cases and not in others? How is

---

4. John 13:23.

Jesus hungry sometimes and then able to go forty days without food at other times? Does Jesus fart, or is that beneath God? Is Jesus naturally talented at everything, or could Jesus be bad at drawing like I am? Is it possible for Jesus, as a human being with a limited vantage point living in a biased culture, to have prejudices? Or does Jesus's divinity demand that he somehow transcends this? If you solve this problem regarding the story of the syrophoenician woman, please email me.

Revelation poses the same question. It is clearly both God-breathed and human-breathed, but how does that work in practice? However one defines *inspiration*, the common denominator is the idea that God used human authors to produce scripture. Scripture is not a set of tablets that descends from heaven to our hands. Rather, it arrives to us today through an incredibly human process:

- In the case of that which becomes the majority of the hebrew scriptures, revelation (live communication from God) is received by one or more persons who then share this revelation orally with the people. It is then passed down orally through countless generations. It is shaped and edited by its tellers. It is written down, edited, and redacted by scribes. These texts are eventually canonized by the community. They are translated into greek in a way that very frequently differs from the older Hebrew texts. The greek translations are quoted by Jesus and the apostles in ways that frequently shift or shade their received meaning. They are translated into countless other languages until they reach us today.
- The Gospels are compiled from accounts of the life and words of Jesus that are originally transmitted orally. Each of the four Gospel authors clearly has their own priorities,

emphases, and motifs as they compile. The Gospels are then shared with the local churches of the first century, and it is not until significantly later that they are canonized, a process that itself involves good intentions and practices but also plenty of harmful values, ethics, and power relations.

- The epistles of the New Testament are utterly occasional documents. They respond to very specific people and the very specific things they have done or failed to do, and their authors make no attempt to hide their biases, theological leanings, and straight-up opinions.

Scripture is undeniably both divine and human. Neither aspect replaces, overcomes, or mitigates the other. Rather, they weave together in a way that is at times stunningly beautiful, at times shockingly insightful, and at other times painfully regressive. Why? Because humans—and human societies and institutions—are at times beautiful, at times insightful, and at times regressive! We might think of scripture as a dialectic—its being always human and always divine may seem like a contradiction, but both aspects, far from fighting against each other, actually depend on each other insofar as revelation, by definition, is communication between God and humanity. And communication, as we know, is never a one-way thing. It is always a process in which both parties contribute meaning and understanding.

In the same confoundingly beautiful way that God chooses to accomplish their *purposes* in the world largely through the *work* of human beings, God chooses to reveal their *thoughts* largely through the *words* of human beings. How amazing is that? Hit a chord on the B3! God can and does depart information and understanding about God's will, character, and intent to human beings in a supernatural way. But that process, like the incarnation of Christ, does not bypass the natural world or human nature but rather *incorporates* them. In all of their beauty. In all of their messiness.

revelation has limits

And because humans have limits, and revelation is human, revelation has limits. Revelation is given through human beings and human cultures. Therefore, we cannot separate theological production from cultural production. There is no sense in which pure, right theology can be deposited to us in unadulterated, sinai-tablet form without the receiving culture mediating and sometimes distorting that theology, based on the limits of its ideas and institutions. All revelation is breathed out by God, but it is then breathed in, and out, and in again by humans. It doesn't arrive before our eyes as scripture before the latter part happens.

Are the cringe-worthy parts of scripture the way they are because humans breathed *in* divine revelation in a way that distorted what was breathed *out* by God? Do they remain with us today not because they are perfect depictions of the fullness of God's nature, will, and actions but rather because they were the way that a limited culture—its immense beauty notwithstanding—was able, at the time, to appropriate the self-revelation of God?

Even the most vibrant and beautiful societies in history have been built on a mix of great ideas, on-the-way-to-good ideas, and busted ideas. There are some aspects of our own contemporary culture and society that make certain aspects of knowing God easier or more reliable (e.g., the place of reason in culture, the availability of information), but there are also many aspects that make knowing God harder and less reliable (e.g., capitalism, exploitation, and all the structures and value systems that support them).

So if scripture were written today, it would contain some ideal theologies and some on-the-way theologies and a whole lot of busted theologies. How could it have been any different during the eras when scripture actually was written? This is unavoidable due to the incarnational and dialectical nature of revelation. We can't avoid it, but what we *can* do is use human reason, and historical analysis, and the guidance of the Holy Spirit to identify, after the fact, which appropriations of revelation—that is, which scriptural ideas and wordings—fit into which category: ideal, getting there, or cringe.

And crucially, this is a process that we must do as *communities*. Every individual is inevitably going to have their own stance on particular texts. But the soundest way to deliberate about these texts is to bring our different reactions and perceptions *together* and let the Spirit speak through the process of discourse, biblical study, and application of anthropological knowledge from science *and* the humanities, which is crucial for sound interpretation of literature.

Is "slaves, obey your masters" (Col. 3:22; Eph. 6:5) busted? Is there little to no revelatory value in this text for us today? Is this a spiritually bankrupt statement written solely to soften the radical politics of Paul[5] and the Gospels in order to accommodate the rulership ethic of empire? Perhaps the community lands here together by consensus.

Or is it on the way? Is there something in the way that the authors are assuming agency in enslaved persons, and/or attributing their ultimate allegiance to God, that demonstrates an ethical progression beyond the dominant values of the context? Is there a principle worth crystallizing here? Perhaps this is where the community lands together. Or the community might decide that yes,

---

5. Colossians, Ephesians, 1–2 Timothy, and Titus are considered deutero-Pauline or pseudepigraphical. They were not written by Paul but likely by folks who came a generation or two after Paul and who considered themselves within the Pauline tradition or school of thought.

Colossians 3:22 is absolutely a betrayal of the antislavery ethic of the movement as stated in Galatians 3:28,[6] *and* therefore its instructive value, and the value of its continued inclusion in our canon, lays not in its being an expression of God's mind but rather in its being a negative lesson in christian accommodation of statecraft.

Furthermore, we can say fairly confidently that there's a reason the 103rd Psalm ("Bless the LORD, O my soul, and do not forget all their benefits—who forgives all your iniquity, who heals all your diseases . . . as far as the east is from the west, so far they remove our transgressions from us") gets quoted a million times per day, and, on the other hand, there's a reason texts that present God as a vindictive, retributive hater don't get quoted quite as much. The cream of the crop rises. The truth cannot ultimately be denied. You will know them— these texts—by their fruit. Thanks be to God.

Throughout the era of the early church, this process of deliberation happens anarchically. Each local church ultimately makes its own determinations about which texts by which to organize its doctrine, theology, and philosophy. They, of course, share resources and consult together confederally about particular texts. But as of yet, there is no bureaucracy that sets a canon and enforces its adoption by local churches. And yet, unfortunately, the final step of canonization—the process of deliberation by which we got the canon we use today—takes place within a statecraft context: the era of the centralized imperial church. So, today, just as scripture itself contains and reflects ethical values and unethical ones, and both the voice of the people and the voice of rulers, so does the history of

---

6. We know that "in Christ there is neither slave nor free" refers not only to spiritual being, leaving one's temporal being enslaved, as if the two could possibly be separated, but rather that Christ makes claims on one's entire existence, and therefore the movement is a renewal of every aspect of life.

canonization. Yes, the canon was formalized during the period of the co-opted church, but that finalization built on the work done during the period of the anarchic church.

And of course, in practice, the canonization process continues today. Every church tradition, and each local church, undergoes its own process of deciding how to engage with scripture. Few of them craft a new formal canon, but all of them craft an *informal* canon— a lectionary that determines which texts get read in worship, or a sermon series plan that determines which books of the Bible get attention, or a leadership approach that emphasizes certain texts and de-emphasizes others, and so on. One good thing we can do is recognize and own this inevitable dynamic and bring it out into the open so that the entire local community can participate in the process.

In all, we have to recognize that statecraft has played a huge part in producing the texts we have and the texts we use—our formal and informal canons—and so has anarchy. The texts that we have, just like our lives, simply cannot be entirely untangled from either. No part of the process of revelation (producing, transmitting, writing, editing, redacting, translating, canonizing, etc.) is free of that rulership-anarchy interplay.

The beautiful thing is that God is still alive and speaking, so we can listen to God as they help us distinguish one from another. When we look at the texts we have today, we know there are the words on the page, and the cultural assumptions behind them (the world behind the text), and the reception in front of them (the world in front of the text). For every text, there are aspects of all three layers that are affirming and beautiful and other aspects that are harmful and distorted. So in our engagement with scripture, we get to consider all three levels, and the many layers within each, in our spiritual deliberation to determine what God is saying through the word for us today.

But wait—we can't just say certain scriptural ideas and statements are misappropriations of God's self-expression and just leave it there, can we? God would not allow something untrue of God to be not only attributed to God once but also preserved and canonized and revered throughout history, would they? God would not allow such a stumbling block to be placed in our path, would they?

I mean, does God "allow" bad things to happen? Does God allow people to misrepresent them? Does God allow people to craft and reify bad theologies?

Yes, Terry, I picked up what you laid down in chapter 3, but this doesn't apply to scripture, right? That's where God draws the line, right?

Hmm . . . can we be certain of this? Or is the question "why wouldn't God intervene to keep this from becoming scripture?" essentially equivalent to "why doesn't a good and all-powerful God prevent bad things from happening?" Is not the assertion "certainly God would intervene to prevent ___ (insert historical event)" theologically equivalent to "certainly God would intervene to prevent ___ (insert cringe idea from scripture) from becoming canonized"?

Where does this leave us with respect to the uniqueness, the *inspired* nature of scripture?

Scripture certainly does sit in a different category from other literature but *not because it's immune to the above questions, not because it stands above and outside the contradictions and conflicts and dialectics of human history, including human-divine interaction. It's in a different category rather because it claims to speak to these questions directly, to deal with them head on, and to offer latencies, analogies, and potentialities for a way forward. To offer a spirit that transcends the letter. To offer a path toward an ideal.* Thanks be to God for such an immeasurable, indescribable gift!

revelation is dialectic

Okay, so the ideal theologies are good as is, and the busted ones we're going to respectfully leave behind, but what about the on-the-way ones? What do we do with those?

This is where the distinction between the spirit of the law and the letter of the law comes in. Sometimes we straight-up misappropriate divine revelation (e.g., God told me to commit genocide;[7] all people from Crete are punk-ass bitches[8]), and other times we absolutely nail it (e.g., God makes me a delicious meal and then makes my enemies watch me eat it;[9] God is love[10]), but other times we receive a word that is good for that moment but not necessarily good or best for all time, even though the *spirit* of it is right and good. To put it differently, revelation is a dialectic of continuity (the spirit remains) and change (the letter does and should shift).

I could write an entire book just listing examples of this, but the most famous ones are the ones Jesus is known for. The homie was constantly getting accused of disrespecting or even desecrating the "law,"[11] was he not? Healing people on the Sabbath, turning over tables in the temple, kicking it with sinners, and so on. What he was doing was, yes, against the *letter* of the laws in question but deeply in keeping with the *spirit* of those laws, much more so than the actions of those who wielded the letter of the law in whatever way they needed to in order to negate its spirit. That's what

---

7. Deuteronomy 20:16.
8. Titus 1:12–13.
9. Psalm 23:5.
10. 1 John 4:7.
11. In chapter 8 we'll discuss the difference between the anarchic covenant of Moses and the statist law into which the temple bureaucracy and the Jewish aristocracy calcified it.

Jesus means when he says he came not to abolish the law but to fulfill it.[12]

And it's not just Jesus who is called on to discern between the letter and the spirit of the law.[13] Peter has to do it too. By the time we arrive to the tenth chapter of Acts, God has already tried on several occasions to get Peter to recognize that gentiles are now included in the church. In order to make it crystal clear for Peter, God sends him the dream of the sheet and the unclean animals who are now clean, one of the raddest stories of the New Testament.

The council at Jerusalem (Acts 15) has to discern spirit from law as well. Paul's letters are basically a several-volume version of him distinguishing between the letter and the spirit of the law. The early church ancestors have to do it. Christians have to do it in every generation through reason, experience, study of scripture, and, most importantly, through listening to the Holy Spirit and to each other.

This is how the church deliberates and recognizes that the *spirit* of the law is that slavery is bad and freedom is good, despite *letters* to the contrary. This is how the church deliberates and recognizes that women pastors and priests are fly. This is how the church deliberates and recognizes that the *spirit* of biblical statements about non-straight sexuality is a concern for individual and communal security and propagation,[14] and for the use of sex to glorify God, and there-

---

12. Matthew 5:17.

13. For more on how the people appropriate christian ethics through deliberation, check out the wonderful Karen Keen and her book *Scripture, Ethics, and the Possibility of Same-Sex Relationships*. (Grand Rapids, MI: Eerdmans, 2018).

14. Which in the time of the Hebrew scriptures takes the form of a heavy emphasis on procreation and rigid patriarchal control over all sexual activity, which are promptly undermined by Jesus, Paul, and others in the NT now that salvation takes the role formerly played by offspring in accomplishing one's immortality,

fore any loving, caring, faithful expression of non-straight sexuality today very much fulfills that spirit.

We do all of this by recognizing that the process of revelation never stops. There is no period, only commas. God breathes it out, and then we breathe it in (initially receiving it), and out and in and out again—sharing it, transmitting it, editing it, translating it, canonizing it, interpreting it, deliberating over it. Revelation is divine, it is human, it is incarnation, it is dialectic, it is limited, it is frustrating, and it is glorious.

Humanity is change and continuity, and so is history, so any process of revelation that incorporates human dynamics cannot result in static theologies that stand for all time but rather in theologies that only achieve their continuity through being reaffirmed, elaborated, reconstituted, and deepened over time.

not making scripture do stuff it doesn't set out to do

Scripture does not need to be, nor does it purport to be, some exhaustive source of all relevant information for understanding the world. When it seems to be claiming to provide us information that we would otherwise look to science or the humanities to provide, we should pause and consider whether or not we are assessing the genre and intent of that text correctly.

For example, we would not and cannot look to science to answer questions such as "is there a God?" and "what is God like?" and "what are God's intentions for humankind?" and "how does God interact

---

and the church takes the role formerly played by the family or clan in providing security.

with humankind?" Those are spiritual questions that categorically defy the limits of scientific inquiry. So if those are the kinds of questions and takeaways that we're engaging scripture with, then we're likely on good footing.

But we *would* look to science to answer questions such as "how old is the world?" and "how does sexuality work?" and the like because those questions *are* within the purview of astrophysics, evolutionary biology, genetics, psychology, and so forth.

Now, when it comes to questions like "is it possible for a human being to give birth to God?" or "did Jesus really turn one cutie's lunch into fish and cheddar bay biscuits for five thousand households?" we come to the point at which spirituality is not anti-rational but superrational. Not against reason but beyond reason. Clearly the texts that ask and answer questions such as these are claiming to be reporting discrete supernatural acts at specific moments of recorded history in a way that confounds and/or interacts with natural, scientifically observable processes such as how pregnancies work or how lunch works.

Now, as y'all know, I do believe in miracles. I *am* part of the *Mystical Negro Masculinity™* movement that recognizes acts of God that can confound or supersede natural limits and constraints. But for me, the beauty of the fish fry on the mount is not so much in the miracle as in its spiritual implications: what it tells us about Jesus, about the kind of abundance he wants for us and is making for us, and about his ability to make a way out of no way.

conclusion

Revelation is anarchic because it happens freely, it happens through cooperation, it is best utilized in a decentralized way, and it is undertaken for the purpose of care. God chooses to communicate with people, who freely choose to listen, record what they take away from that communication, and respond.[15] God and people cooperate in order to reach mutual understanding, to produce records of their communication, and to develop those records over time. Each community must be free to take on this process of its own accord, according to its own needs and context. And God reveals themself to us because they love us and want to have a relationship with us, that we might sublimely come to participate in Godself.

15. You only have to pull this thread a little bit in order to have your mind blown. God chose to remake the world only through the consent and participation of Noah and his family—even if this is an allegory, the theological truth still holds. God chose to reveal their identity and ways through the consent of Moses to lead his people and through his participation in delivering the commandments. God chose to become incarnate in such a way where it could only happen with the consent and participation of Mary. God chose to reveal the beloved community through the consent of the apostles to take risks, take beatings, and ultimately take death on themselves. God chose to create the world so that we could come to consent to participate in the immanent life of God. That's anarchy, fam!

Six

write the vision! make it plain!
anarchy in scripture

Throughout my first summer of seminary, I became obsessed with the imagery and symbolism of the Hebrew temple. I read scholars of the ancient Near East who believed that almost every aspect of the temple's design had spiritual significance. They saw the temple's outer courtyard as representing the inhabitable world, with its washbasin and altar being referred to as the "sea" and "bosom of the earth." They saw the holy place as representing the visible heavens and the stars, with its lampstand of seven lights. They saw the holy of holies as representing the place where heaven and earth met. In all, they believed that the design of the temple was meant to be a reminder of two things. One, the whole world was created as a sacred space. Two, one of humankind's jobs is to continually refresh and reify that idea by extending sacred space across the world.

All of this amounted to a biblical theology of the temple. A biblical theology is a work that takes one motif or concept, looks at how it is treated across a swath or even the entirety of scripture, and draws conclusions based on that survey.

Now, what kind of theology is this book, again? Say it with me—systematic![1] So even though this chapter is going to be in the style of a biblical theology, it is just one piece of a larger argument that makes use of not only ancestral religious literature but also philosophy, logic, cultural studies, etc. to elucidate a particular spiritual path that has been and can be taken by christians past and present. So, keeping in mind everything we just said in the previous chapter about divine revelation and scripture, let's construct a biblical theology of anarchy.

antistatism in the scriptures

I see the second chapter of Genesis as an allegory for an anarchic state of human existence. Two buddies handling their business—getting to name and kick it with all the animals, tending and keeping the garden—which was not toil but rather a chill, therapeutic gardening situation[2]—walking with God, just generally vibing.

Then chapters 3–4 allegorize the emergence of individualism, accumulation, scarcity mentality, competition, and violence. Genesis 6 represents and/or allegorizes the full existential extent of this ethic, as well as God's gracious provision of a hard reset. But then right after they get out of the ark, Noah acts a fool[3] and then gets mad at his son Ham for seeing him acting a fool[4] and consequently curses Canaan, Ham's son and his grandson. Bro! If the problem that led to the flood was that "the wickedness of man was great in the earth, and . . . every intent of the thoughts of his heart was only evil continually" (Gen. 6:5), which allegorically stems from the *curse* of Genesis 3, why would

---

1. I'm hearing this in a Dora the Explorer-style cadence where there's a nice long pause after the question and then we shout out the answer together.
2. The Lord had already "made every tree grow" (v. 9) and had made a mist come up out of the ground to water the plants (v. 6).
3. Genesis 9:20.
4. Insert <Nick Young confused face meme> here.

you then *curse* your grandson out of anger at your son for catching *you* slipping? Did you not just see the rainbow and hear God's promise to never destroy humanity again? Why would you say, "Cool, that's what's up" and then go and try to destroy your grandson?

Then Genesis 11 allegorizes the consolidation of the ethic of chapters 3–4 through a story of the emergence of the state. It's the *institutionalization* of the ethics of individualism, accumulation, scarcity mentality, competition, and violence. It's the domination of the many by the few—make no mistake: you don't build a tower to the heavens out of brick and asphalt in a short period of time without employing exploitative labor—for the sake of centralization ("lest we be scattered abroad over the face of the whole earth") and self-replenishing coercive power ("let us make a name for ourselves").[5] Why worship God or follow a God-given ethic when we can be higher and better than God with "a tower whose top is in the heavens" and thereby become our own gods?

God's intervention against Babel, including by forcing the diversity that human societies were naturally intended to cultivate—but that states expressly prevent as the powerful seek to remake the less powerful in their own image—makes a strong theological statement about God's disdain for rulership, empire, state, and the ethics inherent to them. We hear God say as much again in 1 Samuel 8 when the people ask for a king so that they can be like the other monarchies and empires around them,[6] and God tells Samuel that this is in fact a

5. Genesis 11:4.
6. This is another instance where the historical account of scripture reveals what the ancient near-eastern and Greco-Roman theological aspects of scripture often obscure or even contradict—God is not a coercive ruler. The fact that the people are asking for this is because they don't currently have this. Until now God has been their leader, and by now they've recognized that God is not the coercive, domineering ruler that they think they want: "God's not intervening through violent domination of our enemies like we want. Give us a *real* ruler!"

rejection of God and, by implication, God's ethics. Samuel goes back to the people and says, "Fam, I'm not going to stop you, and God's not going to stop you from doing this. But let me be clear—this dude that you're going to make king is going to *ruin your life*. You want a king to save you from the oppressors, but the king is going to become the new, permanent oppressor."

Actually, let me just remind you exactly what the text says:

These will be the ways of the king who will reign over you: he will take your sons and appoint them to his chariots and to be his horsemen, and to run before his chariots; and he will appoint for himself commanders of thousands and commanders of fifties, and some to plough his ground and to reap his harvest, and to make his implements of war and the equipment of his chariots. He will take your daughters to be perfumers and cooks and bakers. He will take the best of your fields and vineyards and olive orchards and give them to his courtiers. He will take one-tenth of your grain and of your vineyards and give it to his officers and his courtiers. He will take your male and female slaves, and the best of your cattle and donkeys, and put them to his work. He will take one-tenth of your flocks, and you shall be his slaves. And in that day you will cry out because of your king, whom you have chosen for yourselves; but the Lord will not answer you in that day.[7]

---

7. 1 Samuel 8:11–18. The fact that this applies to all states, including and especially modern nation-states, is clear when we think about our "sons and daughters" who have been forced to join the colossally bloated US military, which by its trillion-dollar budget, taken out of our pockets, contributes to the very state-caused poverty that forces many people to join the military, the police, and other self-serving state institutions as the only way to afford college and/ or possibly escape poverty.

Sheesh! How would one not be swayed by these prophetic words from the leading sage of the community? I don't know, but they weren't. They were like, "Cool, cool, cool, that's what's up, that's what's up . . . you done? Okay, great, go anoint a king for us. And make sure he's tall and handsome. No, literally, like, no one else should even come up to his shoulders."[8]

And surprise, surprise—it happens exactly as Samuel predicted. Not just with Saul but with David—yes, beloved David—and Solomon and Rehoboam and all of the kings after the split of Israel and Judah (yes, even the two or three "good"—or, really, less bad—ones).[9]

Esther is one long anti-imperialist narrative. Ecclesiastes is one long tongue-in-cheek roast of Solomon as king and focal point of the apex of the Jewish monarchy/state.[10] Quite possibly the number one motif of the prophetic books is that Samuel was right; kings are bad and states are bad.[11]

The subtext of the New Testament is that not only is the Roman Empire bad, but all states are bad, and therefore the Roman state

---

8. 1 Samuel 9:2. You know that scene where Ron Swanson is at the diner, and he says to the waiter, "I worry that you just heard me say, 'Give me a lot of bacon and eggs' . . . what I said was, 'Give me all the bacon and eggs that you have'?" I feel like this is that, but "I worry that you just heard me say, 'Give us a tall king' . . . what I said was, 'Go find me literally the tallest dude in this nation and make him king.'"

9. Remember when David had a dude killed so that he could cover up the fact that he forced his wife to sleep with him? Remember when Solomon made the people pay for his thousand-person-capacity harem? Remember when things got so whitewashed-tomb that Josiah literally had to rediscover the Torah?

10. A self-roast, if it's written by Solomon, but more likely a roast by an anonymous writer that tradition has named Qoheleth.

11. Who are most of the prophetic invectives directed against? Kings, state bureaucrats—including the king's court and the professional guild of yes-men prophets—temple bureaucrats, and the ruling classes. If the nation had followed the prophets' demands (e.g., economic equity, distribution of power, widespread participation in collective self-governance) to a tee, would the monarchy have survived intact? Most likely not.

should not be replaced by any other typical state, as many wanted Jesus to accomplish, but rather by the kingdom of God, which as we have discussed and will discuss again in the chapter on eschatology is a society where power has been transformed, or perhaps reverted, into care and cooperation.

Now let me pause here and say that many of the US folk reading this might possibly be thinking, "Yes, Terry, I know that monarchies and empires are bad; we learned that in third-grade social studies class. What does that have to do with us and other democratic republics?" Well, yes, I'm sure your third-grade social studies teacher, like mine, made sure to teach you that there is a wide structural and philosophical gulf between empires and modern republics. But I hope I've shown by now, implicitly if not explicitly, that modern republics and traditional empires are much more similar than they are different. They're all societies with a professional governing apparatus that has a monopoly on violence and is used by the ruling classes to control the overwhelming majority of the people.[12] Whenever you have this structure—whether it takes the form of a tribal monarchy; or a sprawling, parasitic empire; or a modern nation-state—it always, always tends toward rule of the many by the few. And we know that the United States, as much as it claims to be a democracy, is actually an oligarchy.

Many of you are already on board with this deconstructive perspective but simply haven't been given a viable constructive alternative. Neither had I for most of my life.

decentralization in the scriptures

Okay, so we've done our very cursory survey of anti-rulership sentiment in scriptural narrative. Now let's look at when and where

---

12. Bookchin, *From Urbanization*, xxv.

decentralization appears. First, let's look at a couple of instances where there is an absence of both rulership and ethics, which, as we discussed toward the beginning, is a situation that slightly overlaps with anarchy structurally but is diametrically opposed to it philosophically.

the era of the Judges in Israel

You probably already knew where we were headed first. Many of you know this—the book of Judges is *wild*. There is some truly bonkers stuff that happens in it. A father kills his daughter in order to keep a very patriarchally stupid vow that he made.[13] Samson captures three hundred foxes, ties their tails together, and sets them on fire in order to burn the fields of an enemy people.

The book ends with quite possibly the most unhinged story in the entire Bible—content warning for the next few sentences: sexual violence. A mob of men from the tribe of Benjamin try to gang rape a levite (a priest's assistant, not dissimilar from a deacon or church staff person today). He gives them his concubine instead; why does a levite have a concubine in the first place? They rape her to the point of killing her, and then the levite cuts her body up into pieces and mails them around to the other eleven tribes to try to get them to turn on the benjaminites. They launch a war against the tribe of Benjamin, but then they feel bad afterward. So they pillage and massacre a city of people who had literally nothing to do with any of this and force its young unmarried women to become wives for four

---

13. Jephthah promises God that in exchange for military victory, when he gets home, he will sacrifice whoever comes out of his house to welcome him home. Even understanding the patriarchal worldview in which all members of a man's household are essentially his property to do with whatever he will doesn't make this any less mind-numbingly stupid and depraved.

hundred of the benjaminites who weren't killed in the civil war. The other two hundred are then allowed to abduct wives from another town in Israel, which also had nothing to do with any of this.

There is a short epilogue that follows the conclusion of this story and wraps up the entire book: "In those days there was no king in Israel; everyone did what was right in his own eyes."[14] Judges is the graphic, detailed demonstration of the truth that decentralization without ethics quickly leads to utter chaos. I still remember one of my favorite professors from seminary saying that Judges is the low point of the Bible, and it shows us the depths to which human society can plummet if we're not vigilant to maintain an ethic of love and cooperation.

Corinth

Let's look at one other example: 1 Corinthians. Many of you know the famous and extremely rad words of chapter 13:

> If I speak in the tongues of mortals and of angels, but do not have love, I am a noisy gong or a clanging cymbal. And if I have prophetic powers, and understand all mysteries and all knowledge, and if I have all faith, so as to remove mountains, but do not have love, I am nothing. If I give away all my possessions, and if I hand over my body so that I may boast, but do not have love, I gain nothing.

> Love is patient; love is kind; love is not envious or boastful or arrogant or rude. It does not insist on its own way; it is not irritable or resentful; it does not rejoice in wrongdoing but

---

14. Judges 21:25, KJV.

rejoices in the truth. It bears all things, believes all things, hopes all things, endures all things: "For now we see in a mirror, dimly, but then we will see face to face. Now I know only in part; then I will know fully, even as I have been fully known. And now faith, hope, and love abide, these three; and the greatest of these is love."

Many people know these lines, but not quite as many people know about the messed-up situation that leads Paul to pen these astoundingly beautiful words. The church in Corinth is a community that, in many respects, has been transformed by the gospel and has thereby, *in principle*, rejected the authority of the empire—in keeping with the example set by the early church in Jerusalem, which we will get to in a moment—and constructed its own mini-society that largely functions apart from the philosophical or structural underpinning of the state. This is good.

The bad part is that the Corinthians have not fully divested from the *practices* of the empire yet. There are factions; there is sexual immorality (e.g., a dude shacking up with his father's wife, folks patronizing the idolatrous and exploitative business of prostitution); there are people suing each other; there are people who aren't being sensitive to other people's dietary needs and preferences;[15] there are groups who eat the Lord's supper before others even get there, leaving nothing for others (some drink so much of that blood of Christ that they get sloppy); and there are those who consider themselves better than others because of the spiritual gifts they have (e.g., the tongues, prophetic abilities, and knowledge that Paul refers to in chapter 13).

---

15. This is more about the religious associations that certain folks have with certain foods than about peanut allergies. But nonetheless these are dietary *needs* that some folks aren't being sensitive to.

This, like the era of the Judges, is decentralization and rejection of bureaucratic authority without the ethic that leads to love and cooperation. And Paul goes *in* on them for this:

- Is Christ divided? Was Paul crucified for you? Or were you baptized in the name of Paul? (1 Cor. 1:13)
- God chose what is foolish in the world to shame the wise; God chose what is weak in the world to shame the strong; God chose what is low and despised in the world, things that are not, to reduce to nothing things that are, so that no one might boast in the presence of God (1:27–29).
- Brothers and sisters, I could not address you as people who live by the Spirit but as people who are still worldly—mere infants in Christ. I gave you milk, not solid food, for you were not yet ready for it. Indeed, you are still not ready. You are still worldly. For since there is jealousy and quarreling among you, are you not worldly? Are you not acting like mere humans? For when one says, "I follow Paul," and another, "I follow Apollos," are you not mere human beings? (3:1–4)
- Some of you have become arrogant, as if I were not coming to you. But I will come to you very soon, if the Lord is willing, and then I will find out not only how these arrogant people are talking, but what power they have. For the kingdom of God is not a matter of talk but of power. What do you prefer? Shall I come to you with a rod of discipline, or shall I come in love and with a gentle spirit? (4:18–21)

But Paul, of course, rebukes them out of love and then culminates his remarks with arguably the greatest love discourse of all time. And the follow-up, 2 Corinthians, seems to indicate that while they did take his message to heart, it was still taking them a while to fully eradicate their former ethic and work out the kinks of this new one.

the return from exile

Now let's look at a couple of examples of proper, though far from perfect, anarchy. First, the twin books of Ezra and Nehemiah. After the long and tragic[16] period of the monarchy and then monarchies in Israel and Judah, the Babylonian empire conquers Judah, destroys its temple, and carries most of the Jewish people into exile. The Persian empire eventually replaces the Babylonian one and takes over the colonization of the Jewish exiles. This time of exile is the period in which we have the novella of Esther, the story of Daniel and his bois Hananiah, Mishael, and Azariah (whose colonized names are Shadrach, Meshach, and Abednego), as well as the lives of many of the prophets.[17]

Then, after seventy years of exile, King Cyrus of Persia feels called by God to let his Jewish underclass return to Jerusalem and rebuild their temple. It's an exciting yet poignant time. The people get home and start to reconstruct their lives, starting with the walls of Jerusalem. "According to their ability," the people pitch in to the

---

16. I should say here that even as the monarchy and its bureaucracy rose in power and scope, the temple continued to function as a centralized bureaucratic authority as well. Because law in Israel was legislated, executed, and adjudicated via religious authority (i.e., we believe our law is from God and that God gave the religious leaders' jurisdiction over it), the political authority was never able to completely replace the temple as the sole central power. Nor did many kings want it to—why take on all that extra work and not get any extra compensation for it?—except Saul; he tried to perform a priestly duty and immediately got replaced by David as result. This is why the prophets drag the corrupt, oligarchical priests as often as they do the kings and royal courts.
17. If you want to get a sense of the vibe of exile in one chapter, read Psalm 137.

funding and labor of rebuilding the temple (Ezra 2:69). Over the course of the narratives of Ezra and Nehemiah, they come together frequently in people's assemblies to work, celebrate, worship, and deliberate (3:1; 3:10–11). The people collectively oversee the projects of workers' guilds (e.g., masons and carpenters). The people appoint Levites to oversee the project (3:8).

The different perspectives and experiences of various groups within the community are given voice: "But many of the older priests and Levites and family heads, who had seen the former temple, wept aloud when they saw the foundation of this temple being laid, while many others shouted for joy. No one could distinguish the sound of the shouts of joy from the sound of weeping, because the people made so much noise. And the sound was heard far away" (3:12–13).

Unfortunately, haters—folks from outside the community—crawl out of the woodwork and cause the work to come to a standstill. For years they bribe Jewish officials and leaders of the reconstruction effort to throw wrenches into the project. Then when King Darius, who was on board with the rebuild, dies and a new king, Artaxerxes, eventually takes the throne, the haters take advantage of the opportunity to snitch on the returnees, talking about "You remember how rebellious and wicked Jerusalem was before y'all so rightfully destroyed it and desecrated its temple, right? Well, there are people here right now trying to rebuild it and go straight back to their old ways, and you *know* they're not going to pay their taxes, and me personally, I just wanted to let *you* know because I respect you so much. All hail the king! Live forever, my guy."[18]

---

18. This is a fair warning for those of us building an anarchic world. There will be haters who try to roll back the various accomplishments we achieve, folks with colonized minds who try to reestablish the methods of rulership even if they themselves don't have access to it.

Xerx Xerx (this is his emcee name)[19] gets the letter, he's pissed, and he orders the construction to stop. The prophets Haggai and Zechariah get the people going again without waiting for official permission. Finally the temple is finished. Everybody gets hype.[20] They throw a bunch of lamb burgers and fatted calf kebabs on the grill. They celebrate the Passover for the first time in two generations.

Nehemiah sees the work forward through more setbacks and more opposition. He demands redistribution of property and resources when the ethics of accumulation and domination start to rear their ugly heads again (Neh. 5). The people's assembly listens to the Torah read publicly for the first time in ages (ch. 8). The priests preach it in a way that everyone can understand (8:3). The people corporately lament the harm that they and their ancestors caused and perpetrated (ch. 9) and come to a consensus on exactly how they're going to do differently in the future: No commerce on the Sabbath so that folks can truly rest and the ethic of accumulation can take a big weekly L. Yearlong sabbatical and full debt cancellation for everyone every seventh year. Everyone tithes to support the work and social services of the community.

The people cast lots to bring one out of every ten persons to live in Jerusalem (11:1), the headquarters of what is now a loose confederation of municipalities, or a league of ancestral clans. The central bureaucracy is not rebuilt along with the walls and temple.

We can see a lot of super-rad anarchy happening in these stories. People's assemblies. Direct participation in decision-making by consensus. Public administration of community projects and resources. Public direction of workers' guilds. Overcoming the haters through

---

19. Imagine his entrance on a feature: "Young Xerx Xerx!"
20. *To the tune of "Tipsy" by J-Kwon*: "Now errbody on the mount getting hype / yes, the courts of the Lord are so lovely."

nonviolent ethical resistance and civil disobedience. Celebration of generational and socioeconomic diversity. Collective observance of communally significant holidays. Anticapitalist policies. Reparations and equitable economic redistribution. All very neat stuff.

Now, we should be sure to say that all of this is happening under the sponsorship and oversight of the Persian empire. The Jewish community is certainly not free, but they are indeed permitted to (re)construct their own political systems as long as none of it conflicts with the general project of the empire. Xerx Xerx said, "As long as that tribute check cashes, you can have your little assemblies and decisions and whatnot, I really don't care." So the postexilic community constructs a society that makes the empire obsolete even as they live within its power. They start out as an anarchic society, but unfortunately the values and ethics of empire gradually win out, and the anarchic community is transformed into a temple-state ruled by the aristocratic priesthood. This setup continues as the Persian empire is replaced by the Hellenistic (Greek/Roman) empire, during which the Jewish temple elite are co-opted by, and rule on behalf of, the romans.[21]

However, even before anarchy gives way once again to state-craft, the postexilic community betrays a true anarchic framework by way of its ethnocentrism. Now, of course, ethnocentrism was part and parcel of living in the ancient Near East. On top of that, if I were just coming out of seventy years of ethnically based trauma, I'd probably come out of that decently ethnocentric too. So it's understandable but still a bummer that the returning folk decide to send away the non-Jewish wives they had married since returning and the

21. For more on Jesus's sociopolitical context, see Richard A. Horsley, *Jesus and Empire: The Kingdom of God and the New World Disorder* (Minneapolis: Fortress Press, 2003).

children they'd had with them. I'm more than willing to accept the idea that it was fine for the community to keep things internal in the first place, but if the deed was already done, no need to add the harm of abandonment to the so-perceived harm of making those bonds in the first place. You just returned from exile, and now you're going to send women and children into exile? Remember, women and children had literally zero autonomy, legal status, or ability to survive without connection to a patriarchal household in the ancient Near East.

It's not dissimilar from what Abraham and Sarah did to Hagar—take the foreign women in—quite possibly against their will or preference—separate them from their culture and community of origin, require them to bear children for them, and then, after a change of heart, send them off alone to fend for themselves. Many of them were likely unable to return to their communities of origin, tainted and defiled in the eyes of their ancestral people.[22]

So it's not perfect anarchy, but there is a lot of good stuff going on here. The same is true of Jesus's community.

the christological dialectic of universality and particularity

Okay, I had to go hard on that section heading real quick for the culture, but, put simply, what I want to talk about right now is this question: how can we speak of christianity as an anarchic, decentralized

---

22. Various biblical scholars have pointed out the irony of the contrast between this perspective on foreign women and that advanced by the book of Ruth. Ruth is a Moabite woman who marries a Jewish man, and both of them are revered for this, both by the community of their time and by their descendants, who celebrate them as close ancestors of King David. But again, it's understandable why Ezra and the postexilic people weren't able to keep this energy.

movement if it hinges on one central leader (Jesus Christ)? Let's talk about how Jesus, the twelve, the seventy-two, and the rest of the lamb of God squad™ organized themselves.

Spiritually and theologically, the movement *is* particular, and you could even say centralized. Jesus Christ *is* God incarnate. As such, he is necessarily theologically central. Like, we worship him. We quite literally center him. This is meet and right so to do.

But politically, socially, and culturally, the movement is *not* particular. Real liberation movements and revolutions are necessarily decentralized. They do not rely on charismatic leadership or authoritarian power structures. Rather, they operate out of a recognition that the movement has to be about spontaneity, equality, and consensus-based decision-making. Everyone is a leader, and no one is a ruler. And all of this is very much true of the Jesus movement. Even the most "central" people in it are *aggressively* ordinary people—the twelve apostles consist of fishermen, a reformed tax collector, and other tradesmen. Several of them never say a word in any of the canonical Gospels. We know very little about those apostles that is historically verifiable, even if there is an incredible amount of extracanonical lore for some of them.[23]

---

23. Have you read the apocryphal *Acts of Thomas*? It's a *treat*. It's a fourteen-act play, and it has everything: love at first sight, which turns out to be unrequited; people fangirling over Thomas and him not having it; a talking donkey who claims to be the great-great-grand-donkey of Balaam's donkey from the book of Numbers; dragons who give "Screwtape Letters"-style expositions on their own demonic activity; apostolic freestyle raps with flute solos; rich theological expositions; powerful martyrdom narratives, and more. In one act the apostle Thomas clowns the king of the region in India where he's settled. The king asks him to build a palace for him, and he's like, "Bet I got you, fam," but then what he actually does is take all the money for the project and give it to those who are poor. And then when the king comes back, he's like, "Well, bro, technically I did build you a palace . . . *in heaven, through my good works that you bankrolled. Lol, got 'em!*" I imagine the ancient Indian church putting on a community theater production of the *Acts of Thomas* every year and having a raging good time.

Jesus sends out the twelve but also the seventy-two, who have power to subdue demons and yet lack purse, bag, and sandals and do not greet anyone on the road.[24] Can you think of any centralized movement led by people who have no money, no swag, no shoes, and no networking skills? The movement operates primarily out of Galilee, which is essentially the boondocks. Jesus is constantly telling people not to tell anyone who he is but just to say instead that the kingdom of God is at hand (i.e., that the movement is here and it's about that time). What kind of central leader does that?

When James and John ask Jesus if they can rule his movement after he's gone, he sets them straight and tells them the least will be the greatest. When Peter gets mad at Jesus for saying he's going to be crucified, and by implication that he won't be a traditionally triumphant messiah *a la* David, Jesus goes in on him too—"Get behind me, Satan!" Apparently Peter didn't get it when literally right before this Jesus told him that he was going to make him the rock of his church. Peter must have heard *rock* as *ruler* when in reality Jesus meant it as *bedrock*. Peter's going to have one of those thankless jobs that no one appreciates when it's done well but everyone notices if it's done wrong. Have you ever looked down at the ground and said, "Hey, ground, you're doing such a good job of being the ground right now— thank you!" I'll bet you haven't. I know I take it for granted. That's what Jesus is telling Peter he's going to be. He will be great insofar as he occupies the bottom and supports everyone else, thanklessly.

Okay, I think I've made my point about the decentralization of the Jesus movement. So how can these two things—the spiritual centrality of Jesus and the self-enacted social decentralization of Jesus—work at the same? It's dialectic time, baby! These two things are far from contradictory—they actually support and rely on each

---

24. Luke 10.

other. We are all *universally* good, loved, and valued, no matter who we are or what we believe, precisely because we have been made such by a *particular* Creator. And those who know Jesus particularly as God do so because we first came to know God as *universal* Love.

Christianity, then, as a *spirituality* is indeed rightfully centered on one person, but the sociopolitical movement of Jesus is quite expressly and repeatedly decentered from any one person. This is true of the movement both during Jesus's earthy life and afterward in the early church. As a matter of fact, there's a lot we could say about how the pneumatology[25] of the early church may well represent and embody this decentralization—Jesus the discrete person removed himself from the picture[26] and then sent the Spirit to dwell in every person and in the movement as a whole.

All of this is to say that the best picture of anarchy in scripture is, of course, Jesus's anarchic movement in the Gospels.

the early church

If the story of Babel is an anti-statist intervention and blessing from God, then Pentecost is not the undoing or reversal of the Babel story, as many have presumed, but rather its fulfillment. Pentecost is the subversion of colonization's dispersal of the Jewish community, the dignifying of the diverse backgrounds and identities that the community now collectively represents. Pentecost is the empowerment of the gospel—the good news of Christ's new order, new ethic, new society—that opens up possibilities for full individual and collective

---

25. Understanding of the Holy Spirit.
26. I love that Jesus was literally in the middle of a conversation with the disciples and then just started floating away, like "I don't mean to cut you off, but this is my ride. Peace out, my homies" (Acts 1:9).

development. That is to say, it ushers in freedom and bestows capacity, whereby we see wonder, miraculous healings, supernatural gifts, and new expressions of wholeness. Pentecost is the welcome of the gentiles into the household of faith and the challenge of both the anti-gentile and the anti-Jewish racism that only serve to pit oppressed people against each other rather than against the empire. Pentecost is the creation of a movement of communities that have seen a viable alternative to the ethics and systems of the empire and have committed to building that different society together.

It's a movement that welcomes baptism requests from Ethiopian court officials, who then bring the movement to their homeland, which means that the gospel has indeed made it to (what at the time represents) the ends of the earth. It's a movement whose members stand up before mayors, councilmembers, and police, exposing their foolishness and the unethical nature of their work. It's a movement of nonviolent direct action against empire and resistance to police repression. Peter and John say to the city officials, "Hmm . . . should we obey you or God? We're gonna go with God on this one" (Acts 4:19).[27] At one point Paul initiates a sit-in: "They beat us publicly without a trial, even though we are roman citizens, and threw us into prison. And now do they want to get rid of us quietly? No! Let them come themselves and escort us out" (Acts 16:37). At several points Paul organizes freedom rides, going to places where he knows, 100 percent, that he and his crew are banned. At another point Paul and Silas pull off the only nonviolent prison break I've ever heard of.

It's a movement of people engaging in debate and discourse in order to reach consensus—in the synagogue, in the public square,

---

27. This is how we know that Romans 13:1–7 is an interpolation. Paul disobeyed authority constantly!

even in the Areopagus.[28] We mostly hear the voice of Paul and the apostles in these instances, but the text indicates that any "lectures" are followed by talk backs whereby many folks reach their own points of access and assent to the movement. These are the folks who then lead the local movement, often in the form of house churches, after the apostles go on to the next town.

It's a movement that empowers people to participate in self-governance and to become the kind of people who can participate even more fully. It's a movement whose leaders, most notably Paul, avoid accumulation of power and cults of personality. Instead they are constantly empowering new leaders, deflecting attention away from themselves and toward the movement, and redirecting power to the people. Paul and Barnabas reject the worship of the people of lystra. Paul works as a tentmaker to support himself. He lives an itinerant, celibate, impoverished life. He appeals to Philemon to emancipate Onesimus, whom Philemon had formerly enslaved, out of love rather than rulership.

It's a movement full of political imprisonments. Paul's is the most prominent, but there are many others. Paul, like Angela Davis a couple millennia later, uses his time as a political prisoner to put together a legal argument not merely to accomplish his own freedom but more broadly to secure the legitimacy of the movement as a whole. Throughout his trial and multiple appeals, he preaches Christ and the movement to the highest religious leaders, to governors, and to emperors. He boldly appeals to their humanity and to whatever ethical overlap they share (Acts 26:27).

---

28. The public square in Athens where folks would gather daily for lively debate and discourse. This was a few centuries after the high point of athenian democracy, but some of the vestiges continued on.

It's a movement that largely rejects punitive and vengeful ethics. Paul goes out of his way to save his incarcerators after the prison ship on which he's being transported is wrecked by a storm.

It's a movement that refuses to be co-opted (Acts 19:13).

It's a movement that welcomes all but appeals especially to the marginalized, particularly women and those who are poor. Thus we have women apostles, evangelists, pastors, and deacons such as Junia, Priscilla, Lydia, and Phoebe, respectively. We have formerly enslaved persons who become coworkers with Paul (Onesimus). We have leaders who come from interfaith households (Timothy). We have a movement full of people who were not "wise by human standards; not many were influential; not many were of noble birth" (1 Cor. 1:26).

It's a movement that comes together in people's assemblies to engage in lively discourse and make tough decisions by consensus— "then the apostles and elders, with the whole church, decided" (Acts 15:22). It's a community of people who place the communal good over their own self-interest—in the case of many, to the point of death.

There are two texts that contain the ethic from which all of the above actions of the early church derive. They are Acts 2:42–47 and Acts 4:32–35, respectively:

> They devoted themselves to the apostles' teaching and to fellowship, to the breaking of bread and to prayer. Everyone was filled with awe at the many wonders and signs performed by the apostles. All the believers were together and had everything in common. They sold property and possessions to give to anyone who had need. Every day they continued to meet together in the temple courts. They broke bread in their homes and ate together with glad and sincere

hearts, praising God and enjoying the favor of all the people. And the Lord added to their number daily those who were being saved.

All the believers were one in heart and mind. No one claimed that any of their possessions was their own, but they shared everything they had. With great power the apostles continued to testify to the resurrection of the Lord Jesus. And God's grace was so powerfully at work in them all that there were no needy persons among them. For from time to time those who owned land or houses sold them, brought the money from the sales and put it at the apostles' feet, and it was distributed to anyone who had need.[29]

I mean, this is anarchy. Creating our own institutions to take care of ourselves and to demonstrate and hasten the obsolescence of the state. Ongoing mutual consent and commitment to a body of shared ethics. Regular fellowship and assembly. Winsome outreach and thoughtful incorporation of new participants. An all-encompassing communal mindset and practice. All property is public. Actually, all possessions are public.[30] The community has one common, sufficient standard of living, and folks are willing to give up some of their own possessions to make that happen—a rejection of accumulation, competition, and self-supremacy. Different subgroups of the

---

29. These are both taken from the NIV.
30. Anarchists reject the idea of private property, which is private ownership of the means of production. This is not to be confused with *personal* property—possessions, ownership of individual goods or products. However, the members of the early church in Jerusalem go so far as to even reject the concept of personal property in order to create a common standard of living, a key tenet of anarchism.

people's assembly are in charge of different projects: distribution of groceries, redistribution of resources that were formerly private property, facilitation of group meetings, organization of spiritual practices, preparation of communal meals, and so on.

It's a beautifully anarchic christianity, and like the early postexilic period, a moment of social reset is what helps it to take off. Not unlike a return from exile to a life that has to be rebuilt from the ground up, the ascension of Christ, along with the descent of the Holy Spirit, totally upends the disciples' world. They have the teachings of Christ, but they're trying to make sense of both the resurrection and Jesus's second farewell. They're waiting together in the upper room, anticipating the arrival of this Holy Spirit that Jesus promised would arrive shortly. They're in the waiting room of a new world.

And then Pentecost comes, and the Holy Spirit descends, and the disciples who had cowardly abandoned Jesus at Gethsemane now rise up with supernatural power and confidence. Signs and wonders make it clear that something new is happening. So they take Jesus's teachings about money, about love, about cooperation, against empire, and they take the power of the Holy Spirit and use all these to create a new way of life. A way of life they believe anticipates and sets the stage for the very imminent return of Jesus, at which point everyone will make the world over by these same principles. And then, after being dispersed by persecution (Acts 8), the church responds not by folding but rather by multiplying and organizing countless villages, towns, cities, and municipalities throughout the Mediterranean world.

Yet, just as with the postexilic community, the anarchy is not yet fully realized. Right after the second text cited above from Acts 4, we have the story of Ananias and Sapphira. This story has always fascinated me because they *did* sell their piece of property and give a significant amount of money to the community—that's pretty good, right? That's more than could be said for the average person of their time and definitely more than could be said for most christians I know today. Yes, the new way of doing things demanded that they bring all of it, but was bringing only part of it so bad as to deserve death?

The key is in verse 4, where Peter says to Ananias, "Didn't it [the property] belong to you before it was sold? And after it was sold, wasn't the money at your disposal? What made you think of doing such a thing? You have not lied just to human beings but to God." I think what Peter is saying is this: "Hey man, look—no one made you join this community. You voluntarily assented to be part of this, and you were at the assembly meeting when we decided to insti-tute this policy whereby folks are required to give *all* of the proceeds from the property sales, which they are strongly *encouraged* but not coerced, to make for the good of the community. I remember that you brought up some concerns during the discussion, after Salome first brought the motion, but I also remember seeing you raise your hand among the 'ayes' when it came time to vote.[31] You know how we do things—votes have to be unanimous in order to pass. So if you had a problem, you should have blocked the vote and taken the motion back to the discussion stage. But you voted yes, so you have to follow through. The way this community works is by people fol-lowing through on what they've committed to do. There's no one that's going to come in and coerce you to do the right thing. We

---

31. Consensus-based decision-making also allows for "stand-asides," where people who cannot yet consent to a decision stand aside to allow the work to go for-ward. Anarchist societies will not always be able to achieve full, wholehearted consent to every proposal, and that's okay. The belief is that with open discus-sion predicated on attentiveness to all concerns, the group will usually be able to find the path forward that is best for all. Even so, occasionally an individual may need to allow their persisting concerns to be noted and filed rather than continue to block progress.

do the right thing on our own because we're capable of motivating ourselves to act right, and we're building a movement that fosters people's ability to do that and rewards them for doing that. We're not bonded by blood, we're not bonded by tribe, we're not bonded by nationality or state or empire—we're bonded by ethical vows we've made to one another. We're bonded by Christ. So it's not so much about the difference between the money you made and the money you gave. It's about the vow you broke—vows that are the bedrock of our fledgling society."

Now, it's important to note that neither the community nor God is said to have caused Ananias or Sapphira's death. It just says they fell down and died. This is important because it reduces, and perhaps even evades, punitive or vengeful connotations for their deaths. Punitive responses to harm or misconduct are expressly not part of an anarchist worldview.

As in Corinth, this story similarly demonstrates the time and work required for the full effect of the gospel to set in and fully transform the people and the systems they build together. The same gap appears again in the next chapter, when there is a conflict between those from the diaspora and those from the homeland concerning inequitable care for each group's respective widows. This leads to the ordination of the first deacons, who are then tasked with overseeing equity in the distribution of resources.

conclusion

Anarchism as a systematic political philosophy has been around for less than two hundred years. But anarchy as a rejection of rulership has been around since the emergence of rulers and the state, and it has presented itself in some form in virtually every society across history. The societies described in scripture, as well as the communities that produced scripture, are thankfully no exception. Once we are equipped with an anarchist hermeneutic with which to read scripture, we can do a survey of where anti-rulership sentiment and practices are present, and we can learn much whether we zoom out to the forest (looking at broad trends) or zoom in to the trees (interpreting specific stories).

What I see when I look at anarchy in scripture is a picture similar to what I've seen in anarchist philosophy. I see that anarchy, as we've mentioned, is the best way to organize and cultivate human society. It does not inherently prevent all human problems, but it *does* give us the best chance of understanding and dealing with human issues effectively. The early church in Jerusalem, anarchic as it is, still has to deal with the question of what to do with their (former?) oppressor (Paul), who is now trying to join them (and lead them?). There are still major beefs that are proving hard to resolve (e.g., Peter versus Paul). But anarchy allows the early church to tackle those issues within an exciting, vibrant, beloved community rather than the mire of ever-reshuffling forms of exploitation, where many other communities around them are.

Seven

this is the way[1]
anarchy in church

church history in three pages

The first three centuries of christianity continue very much in line with the situations described above in Jerusalem, Corinth, and all the places where the apostles raise up leaders to lead local churches. The anarchic setup persists. There is no central bureaucracy that administers the christian community as a whole. It operates confederally, not unlike a league of churches. Each church freely associates with other churches, sharing resources—including letters written by Paul and other apostles and evangelists, which they circulate to each other—debating and consenting to matters of doctrine and practice, and engaging in mutual aid (e.g., the collection for the church at Jerusalem, which Paul references in multiple epistles). There are bishops who are considered to have received their authority from

---

1. All I want is for Disney to acknowledge that it borrowed this from us (Acts 9:2, 19:9, 22:4, 24:14). Preferably in the style of a YouTube apology video featuring Din Djarin and Din Grogu. And they need to cite their sources for the immaculate conception of Anakin too.

the apostles and who oversee regions and all of the churches within them. But these bishops exercise stewardship and care, not dominion or rulership, and as of yet there is no bishop of bishops, no pope or papal bureaucracy, to whom everyone submits and reports and from whom church affairs proceed. Priests and deacons oversee individual churches, and laypeople run them. They found orphanages, hospitals, and mutual aid programs (e.g., to the point where widows are not only taken care of but seem to have become a lay order in the church not dissimilar from a noncloistered monastic order today).[2]

Throughout this time, the Roman Empire cycles through periods of violent repression, less direct subjugation, and disdainful tolerance of christians, largely depending on who is emperor at the time. During the more violent periods, many christians are given the choice to either recant their beliefs or be executed. These are the martyrs represented by the souls that John sees under the altar in Revelation 6. It's a scary time.

Then, in the fourth century, the emperor Constantine breaks rank with his predecessors and makes christianity the official religion of the Roman Empire. The upside of this is that official persecution of and violence toward christians stop. The downside is that by and large, christianity fairly quickly goes from being an anarchic, ethical, radical religious movement to being a bureaucratic, corrupt, status-quo-keeping state institution.

Throughout history, states have responded to radical movements by repressing them, ignoring them, or co-opting them. The Roman Empire tried both of the first two options intermittently throughout the first three centuries of christianity, and then Constantine realized that the third would be much more effective. Constantine and

---

2. Cf. 1 Timothy 5.

his predecessors heard the christians saying "Jesus is Lord," and at first they were like "oh, hell, no—I'm Lord." But after fighting it for centuries, after martyring tons of people and still not being able to snuff christianity out, Constantine was like "Forget fighting it; I'm going to co-opt it. The phrase 'Jesus is Lord' doesn't bother me if 'Jesus is Lord' and 'Caesar is Lord' are functionally the same statement." And thus the empire defeats the most anti-imperial claim of christianity—Jesus is Lord—not through repression, not by waiting out christianity's expected natural demise, but through co-optation.

The cross was originally a symbol of Rome's power to crush any who challenged its supremacy. Then Jesus subverts the cross into an anti-imperial symbol that evokes the naked ugliness of state rulership and the greater power of nonviolent love. Tragically, a few centuries later, the church allows Rome to revert the cross back into a symbol of empire as its soldiers murder, pillage, and dominate with crosses on their shields. Empire has co-opted the church.

The marriage of church and empire was a very, very, very bad thing. I don't think I need to list examples here. Nevertheless, radical christianity was not snuffed out entirely. Many local churches, from the fourth century on, continued to do their best to live as the early church had. Many churches and church networks found various ways to subvert or break free from the power of Rome. The church continued to spread to lands outside of the imperial reach of Rome. Monasteries and monastic orders, the saving grace of the medieval church, were communes that operated mostly apart from outside rulership—functionally, at least. Reformers rose up here and there, calling christians back to radical religion and posing serious challenges to ecclesiastical authority. The Protestant movement gave opportunity for church to be organized and practiced outside of the authority of centralized bureaucracies but also quickly led to new co-optations of faith by newly "Protestant" states. Just as imperial christianity[3] was and is the bedrock of colonization, enslavement, and capitalism, radical christianity was and is the engine of many liberation movements in the United States, Latin America, and various other colonized regions around the world. And it can and does continue to be so today.

anarchy in church today

Deconstruction. This is one of the most hot-button, resonant, and often cringey words in the American church context right now. We have "exvangelicals," church exoduses, and church hurt. We have folks exploring other spiritualities, including agnosticism and atheism, which are certainly spiritual meaning systems in themselves, and folks wandering between christian traditions. There is a lot going on right now in the realm of spiritual migration.

I am an anarchist christian who has migrated[4] through white evangelicalism, Black evangelicalism, conservative white presbyterianism, white anglicanism, Black anglicanism, and progressive white mainline-ism[5] to arrive where I am today. Each tradition has made lasting positive contributions to the development of my spirituality.

Evangelicalism taught me how to enjoy scripture and how to make spirituality fun and exciting. The mainline taught me that God

---

3. That is, the marriage of christianity and the state, not least the white supremacist abomination and mockery that has characterized much of "christian" expression in US history.

4. Migration studies can be a helpful way to frame these issues. For example, migration is often caused by upheaval, oppression, or war. Certainly much of our spiritual migration is caused by spiritual upheaval, oppression/abuse, and conflict that could surely be described as spiritual warfare.

5. *Mainline* is a term used for more formally liturgical historically white protestant traditions such as the lutheran, episcopal, and presbyterian churches. I wish I could say the term comes from "Jesus on the mainline / tell him what you want," but unfortunately the etymology is not quite as rad as that.

is shaping me through the habits and structures of spirituality even when it's not fun or even emotionally resonant. The Black church taught me how to bring every part of who I am, boldly, before the throne of grace. The anglican tradition introduced me to the Book of Common Prayer and to prayer-writing as a spiritual practice. The progressive church showed me how to do justice and love mercy, how to practice that St. James kind of religion—to look after orphans and widows in their distress. I am so, so grateful for all of these spiritual homes, however temporary they were.

Some of these traditions also hurt me. Conservative churches hurt me with, among other things, their harmful ideologies. Mainline churches hurt me with, among other things, their bureaucratic arrogance and negligence; that's about as simply as I can put it. What all of the hurt really comes down to, though, is authoritarianism. Theological and ecclesial rulership.

In my theological training and in church work, I have encountered countless people with similar ongoing stories of spiritual sojourn. Along the way I've tried and failed to make sense of it and find meaning in it. The nascent meaning I've found can be presented through the lens of the building blocks of anarchy: decentralization, freedom, solidarity, and revolution.

The ecclesial destabilization and **decentralization** effected by the spiritual exile and sojourn of many people, while often resulting from things that are harmful, can be good. The church was always meant to be decentralized, flexible, mobile, and fully opposed to accumulation and rulership. The experience of spiritual sojourn can be channeled into the cultivation of decentralized spiritual communities similar to those of the early church.

The theological **freedom** effected by the spiritual exile and sojourn of many people, while often resulting from things that are harmful, can be good. It can lead to new or rediscovered theologies and theological processes that are poised to breathe life into a dying church.

The spiritual **solidarity** and cooperation effected by the spiritual exile and sojourn of many people, while often resulting from things that are bad, can be good. The Evolving Faith network[6] is just one example of this, as are the many communities that have been built up around doxologically innovative projects such as Black Liturgies, Liturgies for Parents, and the Porter's Gate. These forms of solidarity and cooperation can replace the old bonds of class, tradition, and power that largely bound the dominant church of the American yesteryear.

Spiritual transformation is a personal and public **revolution**. Individually we are revolting against spiritual conditions that have oppressed and limited us, and we are being made new into beings whose spirituality is liberative. Communally we are revolting against spiritual traditions and communities that have oppressed and limited us, and we are being made into new spiritual communities whose practice and work are liberative.

The old church is dying out. The old ways are demonstrating their obsolescence. Yet many seek to put new wine in old wineskins. The spiritual sojourn situation is proof that the harvest is plentiful, but the workers are few. Let us take a close look at the wine so that we may come to know what new wineskins we must create for it.

conclusion

In whatever spiritual spaces we find ourselves, in whatever spaces we create, we are more than capable of clearing the weeds of rulership

6. Shoutout to Jeff, my seminary orientation leader; and Kenji, my platonic soulmate. ♥

out of the soil of the church to make room for the seed of the Spirit. We are more than capable of cultivating pastors and spiritual leaders in general who lead through care, not through domination. We are more than capable of creating horizontal decision-making structures that rely on congregational participation, discourse, and consensus. Our churches are more than capable of remaining connected and accountable to each other through free, nonhierarchical regional associations. We've done it before, with God, and we can certainly do it again.

Anarchy was the predominant organizational form of the early church. It was widely attested even after the imperial institutionalization of the church. And it lives on today in various traditions as an invitation for us to foster cooperation, care, and personal and collective faith development.

Eight

remix the covenant

anarchy in community

One of the things I love about anarchism is that it is a challenge to all dimensions of our lives. Making rulership obsolete is something we can do on a communal scale, on an interpersonal scale, and even on an intimate *intra*personal scale. We've discussed some of the political ways to do this (chs. 1–2), some of the spiritual ways to do this (chs. 3–6), and now in this chapter (and the previous) we're looking at some of the social ways to do this.[1] So now we ask, *how do we abolish rulership in our relationships?*

virtue ethics

In chapter 5 we talked about how Jesus, the apostles, and the church throughout its history have all had to use spiritual discernment to distinguish between the letter of the law and the spirit of the law. We can call this *virtue ethics*—making decisions about the best ways

---

1. But, of course, the social is spiritual, the spiritual is political, the political is social, these are not mutually exclusive categories, etc.

to act based on the virtues (spirit) and/or vices from which those intentions come within us and that those actions cultivate within us. For Jesus, to not heal on the Sabbath could've been argued to be in keeping with the letter of the covenant, but it would've been out of keeping with the spirit of the covenant—namely, to give people rest. The virtues at stake here are care and attentiveness for Jesus and dignity and freedom for the person healed. To not heal would have cultivated the opposing vices.

This is why Jesus says that we were not made for the Sabbath, but rather the Sabbath was made for us (Mark 2:27). In other words, a particular conduct prescription is only so good as the virtue it cultivates. If it's not cultivating virtue, we need to examine how we're applying it or recognize that in a new context, different from the one it was originally written for and applied to, it is no longer accomplishing its inherent spirit and therefore needs to be replaced with a different instruction that does. And is this not what Jesus does? That part where he gives us a new commandment, one that sums up all the law and the prophets?

the structure of a covenant

A classic tenet of anarchism is the abolition of law. No states = no law. Therefore, many anarchists reject christianity because it seems to be, and often presents itself, as founded on various *laws*. And yet when we say the word *law* today, we refer to a set of conduct guidelines legislated by the state and enforced by violence, coercion, or the threat thereof. This is not at all what Jesus instituted, nor is it what Moses instituted. What God gave the people through Moses was not at all *law* in the sense of the word today. It's more properly understood as a *covenant*. Therefore, when Jesus *fulfills* the mosaic tradition, he's not (re)establishing statist law but rather renewing, remixing, and remastering the covenant of the Hebrew people.

Many schools of anarchism propose the covenant to set and maintain ethical standards of conduct after the obsolescence of the state. A covenant is an articulation of various communal ethical principles to which people voluntarily and freely consent. This is what the "law" of Moses is.

When the psalmist says they love the law, are they talking about state legislation? No, they're talking about God's ways. They're talking about the covenant that distills the ways of God for human beings to follow. The original mosaic law, similarly, is not at all a law in the sense that we use the word today. It is not a set of injunctions passed by legislators, interpreted by courts, and enforced by police. It's a statement of God's ethics and guidelines for how the people can live by them. It's a covenant.

Now, does this covenant eventually get calcified in Hebrew tradition into legislative prescriptions determined and enforced by the temple and palace bureaucracies? Yes, certainly. But the original mosaic law is an anarchic covenant. Far from naturally being the voice and tool of rulers, it expressly prohibits human rulership, teaching that God is the people's sovereign. Instead, it instructs the people to collectively deliberate on how to interpret the principles of the covenant in instances of conflict over civic conduct. They are to do this with the leadership of judges who have the authority of expertise and experience, not the authority of bureaucratic rulership over the people.

Richard Horsley lays out the structure of the covenant in a rad way in his book *Jesus and Empire*. He looks at the original giving of the covenant on sinai (Ex. 20), the covenant renewal ceremony (Josh. 24), and the elaborated teaching in Deuteronomy to identify the basic covenant as having a three-part structure:

1. A statement of God's deliverance of the people from bondage in Egypt
2. The Ten Commandments
3. Blessings and curses in future life as a result of keeping or not keeping the commandments

Put differently, the mosaic covenant consists of:

1. A statement of God's deliverance that evokes the gratitude and obligation of the delivered to keep the ensuing principles
2. Principles of solidarity with God and with one another
3. A description of what life looks like if the covenant is followed and what life looks like if it's not

So the covenant consists of an identity narrative, ethical principles, and a general statement of the outcome of following versus not following those principles. Why? Because first, we have to know who we are and where we come from in order to know why we do what we do and why we believe what we believe. Then we state what we believe. Lastly, we paint a picture of what it looks like for us to live in accordance with our beliefs and what it looks like to not. This is the basic structure of a covenant.

Note that the covenantal principles—in this case the Ten Commandments—are not injunctions or prescriptions for particular situations but rather general ethical conventions. The Hebrew scriptures certainly do have contextual prescriptions (e.g., what to do if your ox accidentally kills another person's ox), but these are applications of the covenant, not the covenant itself. Specific injunctions and prescriptions are static. They are context-dependent, by definition. They cannot be universal. Ethical principles, on the other hand, can be universal precisely because they are dynamic, adaptable, and non-context specific.

The applications of the principles are by definition time-bound. They must be revisited and rearticulated by every generation. But the spirit of the law remains even as the letter of the law rightfully changes. For this reason a covenant provides the spirit of a community's ethics, from which the people can collectively derive specific applications as needed.

the anarchy of the christian covenant

So when Jesus says he's come not to abolish but to fulfill the law, he's very much reupping the identity statement, ethical principles, and sanctions of the mosaic covenant. But he's applying those principles in a way that is proper for and appropriate to his context. "You have heard it said, but I say unto you"—"this is how our ancestors applied these principles in their context, and this is how we should apply them in ours."

So Jesus fulfills the mosaic covenant by *renewing* it. Jesus's renewed covenant follows the same three-part structure: identity statement, ethical principles, and consequences.

First, Jesus gives the people a new identity statement:

Blessed are the poor in spirit, for theirs is the kingdom of heaven. Blessed are those who mourn, for they will be comforted. Blessed are the meek, for they will inherit the earth. Blessed are those who hunger and thirst for righteousness, for they will be filled. Blessed are the merciful, for they will receive mercy. Blessed are the pure in heart, for they will see God. Blessed are the peacemakers, for they will be called children of God. Blessed are those who are persecuted for righteousness' sake, for theirs is the kingdom of heaven. Blessed are you when people revile you and persecute you and utter all kinds of evil against you falsely on my account. Rejoice and be glad, for your reward is great in heaven, for in the same way they persecuted the prophets who were before you.[2]

Just as "I am the Lord your God who brought you out of Egypt" is an identity statement for the mosaic covenant, so are the beatitudes the identity statement for the christian covenant. Jesus is making it clear what kind of people are part of his movement, whose blessing and favor they have, and what is theirs as a result (the kingdom of God).

Jesus moves from this new identity statement to a series of sayings that rearticulate and re-up the timeless ethical principles of the mosaic covenant. Over the next couple of chapters, he gives teachings on anger, marriage, loyalties, nonviolent resistance, love, mutual aid, spiritual practices, finances, where to look for security, not judging others, having an abundance mentality (ask, seek, knock), the Golden Rule, doing what's right rather than what's popular, knowing people by their actions rather than their appearance or status, and doing the actual work rather than being a poser. All of these teachings revive and advance the ethical principles of the mosaic covenant.

It's the same principles, but now it's a higher bar for application, given that the social and political bar is higher now too. The bar is higher all around because now we're putting together an anarchic community centered around the incarnate God-man who helps us to become divinized human beings.

You have heard it said, "do not commit adultery," but I say to you do not even lust. Like, literally, if your right eye causes you to sin, rip it out of its socket. You've heard it said, "do not swear falsely," but I say to you do not swear at all. Let your yes be yes and your no be no—don't appeal to any power besides your own in order to put force or reliability behind your own commitments.

And the most famous one—you've heard it said, "it's fine to return proportional violence for violence—an eye for an eye." But I say to you never engage in violence of any kind. Instead, engage in nonviolent direct action—turn the other cheek, give your cloak as well, go the second mile—in other words, confront your enemy with your humanity by doing something unexpected that reasserts your humanity, dramatizes the injustice of their actions, and highlights the righteousness of your movement.

After giving these new articulations of ageless ethical principles, Jesus concludes the Sermon on the Mount—the dispensation of the renewed covenant—with consequence statements, a description of how things will look when we follow the covenant and how they'll look when we don't. It's the parable of the house built on the sand and the house built on the rock. What I love about this framing is that it gets away from traditional "my suffering is God punishing me for my sins" theology. The parable makes it clear that bad things (storms) will come either way—what makes the difference between collapsing and standing firm is the structures we have built for ourselves. In other words, bad things are not curses from God for unrighteousness. They're part of living in this world as it is currently, and we can't control them, but thankfully we can always control our own ethics, which is what ultimately determines whether we collapse in the face of rulership or whether we stand firm.

God is not a coercive ruler, and therefore God does not rule through the tool of law. Instead, God helps people craft communal covenants into which they may enter freely and by which they can commit to living together ethically. This is why Matthew's recounting of the Sermon on the Mount, the giving of the renewed covenant, ends with this: "Now when Jesus had finished saying these things, the crowds were astounded at his teaching, for he taught them as one having authority, and not as their scribes." The people were astounded because they knew exactly what Jesus was doing. He was not giving them a bunch of isolated one-liners. He was not merely preaching a cool sermon that they could forget about the next day. He was dispensing a new covenant, one that the scribes and the other aristocrats could never come up with because they were about finding loopholes in the mosaic covenant, not about renewing it in order to apply its timeless principles of cooperation and care to their context.

While covenants consist of origin statements, ethics, and sanctions, they often also come with words of commitment through which people vow to live by them. The Hebrew people made this vow to enter into and reaffirm their communal covenant: "Hear, O Israel: The LORD is our God, the LORD alone. We shall love the LORD our God with all our heart, and with all our soul, and with all our might."[3]

Simple. Comprehensive. Hard.

The early christian community said words of commitment to enter into and reaffirm their covenant as well: "Our father, who art in heaven, hallowed be thy name. Thy kingdom come, thy will be done, on earth as it is in heaven. Give us this day our daily bread, and forgive us our debts, as we forgive our debtors. And lead us not into temptation but deliver us from evil. For thine is the kingdom, and the power, and the glory, forever and ever. Amen." Understood comprehensively, this is not only a prayer but also a vow by which we commit ourselves to Jesus Christ's movement and to its particular local community of which we are a part. We're articulating our recognition of who we are and what we do:

---

3. Deuteronomy 6:4.

- Who is this covenant with? God.
- Whose kingdom are we about? Caesar's or Christ's? Satan's or God's? The kingdom of violence, coercion, and exploitation? Or the kingdom of love?
- Whose will is supreme? Our own or the will of God, which is that of love?
- Is it only in heaven? No, it's on earth too. We don't separate ultimate truth from the temporal realities of civics and politics. We don't get to wait until the by and by to do what Jesus taught; we have to—we *get* to—do it now.
- Everybody gets their daily bread. Everybody eats. Everybody has their needs met. Everyone has a common sufficient standard of living. We do this the only way possible—through mutual aid.
- Cancellation of all debts—financial, relational, etc. We don't oppress each other in order to try to make up the money that the rulers are stealing from us.
- We don't flirt with the devil. We flee from the devil. We make no peace with oppression. We make no compromise with the state.
- And we know who has the power and the glory. And consequently in all of this, we are more than able. Forever.

Let's remember what we're doing when we say the prayer Jesus taught us. We're renewing the covenant. We're assenting to a statement of who we are, what we do, and what the world looks like if we do it. And this covenant is written on our hearts, not on stone tablets.[4] We do right because it's our ethics, not because written legislation forces us to.

---

4. Jeremiah 31:33.

covenantal conflict mediation

So this is the covenant. What do we do when members of the community fall short of it? Jesus shows us exactly what to do in Matthew 18:

> If your brother or sister sins, go and point out their fault, just between the two of you. If they listen to you, you have won them over. But if they will not listen, take one or two others along, so that 'every matter may be established by the testimony of two or three witnesses.' If they still refuse to listen, tell it to the church [assembly]; and if they refuse to listen even to the church, treat them as you would a pagan or a tax collector.

Note the restorative nature of conflict mediation in Jesus's movement. Harmed and harm-doer figure out what accountability and justice look like together. The community participates in deliberation. And if anyone refuses the accountability of the community, they have thereby, by definition, voluntarily chosen to leave the community. No hatred, no punishment, no coercion, no violence. When Jesus teaches his followers to forgive "seventy times seven," he's not saying that we must forego accountability. He's saying that we must give up our (felt) "right" to hate and/or judge the one who has harmed us, instead trusting the community to properly, with God's guidance, handle mediation, accountability, and justice.

The word translated "church" here is *ekklesia*—the assembly of the people. Jesus is calling for the local chapters of the movement, the local communities that together make up the beloved community, to adjudicate conflict through a people's assembly that makes decisions based on the ethical covenant they have freely entered into with one another. This is what anarchists do.

REMIX THE COVENANT   131

the conflation of covenant and law

Rulers like to present themselves as standard-bearers of timeless ethics, when in reality they distort and twist ethics in order to craft *law* as the coercively enforced articulation of their own anti-ethical, antisocial practices. Politicians today present themselves as "tough on crime," or as "law and order" candidates, as protectors of "family values," and other nonsense. And yet of course they obviously, in reality, contribute to a machine that creates harm, disorder, and dissolution of kinship.

The Judean aristocracy presented itself as protectors of the ancient Hebrew ethical covenant. And yet, as Richard Horsley points out, "contrary to the christian stereotype of the Pharisees as rigorists on the law, their contemporary opponents who wrote the dead sea scrolls labeled them 'smooth interpreters' because they were lax accommodators of the law to their own interests."[5] *Hmm, the covenant teaches mutual aid, but that keeps us from accumulating power and resources, so let's make it unlawful to heal on the Sabbath, and let's create loopholes that allow people to not have to cancel debts.*

Christians today often reject the mosaic covenant precisely because of the Pharisees ("If that's their whole thing, then I really don't want to be associated with it"). But this is exactly what rulers want us to do. They want us to conflate ethics with legislation and then reject both, which gives them undisputed reign over both. They want us to hand them the pen to rewrite ethics however they want to.

Rulers associate themselves with ethics as a misdirection to avoid scrutiny of their actual practices *and* to cast aspersions on the good ethics of the people they exploit. Rulers around the world calling themselves

---

5. Horsley, *Jesus and Empire*, 121.

socialists. Rulers in the United States calling themselves democrats. The Pharisees succeeding in getting us to believe that their law is the covenant, when in reality their law is precisely the *negation* of the covenant. It's all the same playbook. They're legalists, yes, but they're rigorists to their own calcified statist law, not to the living ethical covenant of the people.

When we conflate ethics and law, we play right into the rulers' game. When we rely on written injunctions and prescriptions for our ethics rather than on active deliberation, we play right into the rulers' game. It's super easy for the rulers to control interpretation of written texts. It's much harder for them to control communal deliberation and consensus over how to apply timeless ethical principles to a community's context.

Let's look at an example from scripture. The Judean aristocracy tried to trap Jesus by asking him if it was lawful for a man to divorce his wife. Now, the ancient text said yes but out of a context in which to say a man could divorce his wife was actually a progressive statement. It meant that a man had to provide a certificate of divorce, which meant there were certain duties a man had in order to make sure that a divorced woman was not left destitute, as opposed to previously when men could abandon their wives at any time for any reason.

So the way to apply that principle in Jesus's context was to say no because in Jesus's context, elites would divorce and remarry to consolidate their control of land and other resources. In both cases it's about lifting up women.

In our context today, the way to apply that principle would be to say, "Yes, it is acceptable to divorce if there has been a breach of the marriage vow. People do not need to stay in abusive relationships; to force them to do so would be to violate the basic ethic of care." Within anarchy, the people's assembly comes together to make these kinds of deliberations. To deliberate over timeless ethical principles, contained within our covenants, in order to determine proper contextual application.

Jesus provided a new and ultimate covenant that rendered legislation unnecessary. He showed us how to organize in anarchic communities and make decisions together in people's assemblies. He showed us how to handle conflict collectively. All of this makes law obsolete. No more managing harm with harm. No more frozen legislation posing as ethics but actually enforcing the ways of rulers. Jesus came to demonstrate that actually people are good, and therefore cooperative societies are possible, and within those societies, people can enter into ethical covenants, whereby law is unnecessary and regressive.

a law framework applied to sexuality

Let's look at another example of the difference between law and ethics, this time in a modern context. Like many christians—perhaps like you, reader—I was raised in a community that applied a heavy law framework to dating and sexuality. Don't have sex before marriage. Don't date someone who's not a christian. Don't front-hug a girl—christian side hugs all around. Don't masturbate. Little talk of ethical principles, much talk of particular conduct injunctions set down from the lofty heights of Focus on the Family, the 700 Club, Billy Graham, etc.

Rulers create law either by fixing their own particular interpretation of codified ancestral principles or simply by creating new prescriptions of their own. The Judean aristocracy did both—they interpreted the ancient texts in the way that was most beneficial to them, regardless of how ethical these applications were, and they also wrote new prescriptions that they quickly made binding.

In the case of our youth-group guys' nights, we received the sage wisdom of some evangelical ruler(s) who had decided that the correct and mandatory interpretation of "do not commit adultery" (a solid principle) or "do not fornicate" (a word that is not defined in scripture) was "do not have sex as an unmarried person." They had also added several new laws that could hardly have been said to derive directly from the text (e.g., no masturbation, no sexual expression of any kind outside of marriage).

At a certain point, however, evangelical thinkers began to realize that it was not enough to give people negative laws—don't do this, don't do that. They also had to give them positive commands. Enter the plethora of christian guides to dating and sexuality, including *Every Young Man's Battle*, *For Young Women Only*, and, by far the most popular and culturally impactful, *I Kissed Dating Goodbye*. Its message was this:

> Casual dating is worldly and sinful. What you need to do is court. You need to meet someone, pine after them, and then, only when you are *certain* that you can see yourself spending the rest of your life with them, do you begin to court them. The whole process shouldn't take long because God will have been doing the same work in them that God was doing in you. You'll talk a few times, meet the parents, ring by spring, nuptials by November. And then you will know unspeakable romantic and sexual satisfaction, awarded to you as a prize for your chastity and your rejection of worldly dating in favor of Christian courtship.

In recent years, there have appeared countless books, Instagram captions, Medium blog posts, and podcast episodes about how all of this is foolishness. The author himself recanted the book. We don't need to rehash all of that. What I do want to talk about is how this demonstrates the practical difference between a law framework and a virtue ethic.

First of all, a law approach to ethics does *nothing* to develop a person's discernment, self-mastery, or virtue. When I tell you that *I Kissed Dating Goodbye was* my sex education, even though I went to public school, I need you to understand that I finished high school—really college, honestly—with little to no sense of what sexuality was, what it was for, how it functioned physiologically, and how to engage in it caringly and responsibly other than "it's for bonding with your spouse and for making babies." I avoided porn and lust out of sheer fear of the presumed wrath of God, not out of a clear, comprehensive, rational, ethical understanding of the inherently exploitative nature of porn and its industry or the way that lust objectifies women. In other words, I had fear-based self-restraint, but I lacked ethical self-mastery. And I had no sense of what virtue sexuality could cultivate beyond marital bonding and procreation. What about self-awareness? What about restfulness and contentedness? What about communication, cooperation, teamwork, extension of one's self for another person's nurture?

Law also creates binary all-or-nothing frameworks. Either you're right or you're wrong. Either you're good or you're bad. You're either single and functionally aromantic or you're courting and functionally married; in the courtship framework, you're basically engaged as soon as you take one step forward. You're either a functionally asexual being or experiencing divinely sanctioned marital sexual bliss. You're blissfully sexually ignorant (single) and then wondrously sexually all-knowing (married). You're pure on your wedding day, or you're hopelessly tainted. You, on your first romantic foray ever, marry the soulmate God made just for you, or you marry the wrong person. Yeesh.

virtue ethic applied to sexuality

I'm now a hard-core virtue ethicist with respect to sexuality, which also means I'm a very nonbinary thinker. Sex and sexuality themselves are morally neutral. It is the context that makes them more or less ethical. Many romantic or sexual expressions can be ethically positive and healthy, if undertaken with care, respect, equity, and understanding. What makes them more or less ethical is simply the degree of virtue that generates them and the degree of virtue they in turn cultivate. Now, are there certain relationship setups that structurally cultivate virtue better than others? Absolutely. I do believe that long-term relationships are the best structure for developing deep care, respect, mutual knowledge, mutual aid, and love mainly because virtue is enriched by time, commitment, and intentionality. But I do not believe that other relationship structures are inherently unable to operate by or foster these virtues. They will simply require extra intentionality, attentiveness, and care to account for the lesser quantities of time, mutual knowledge, and commitment.

the abolition of the nuclear family

As you might imagine, I would make these claims about not only romantic relationships but all relationships. Communication, commitment, and intentionality are virtues that create a real, felt dynamic of belovedness and support in any kind of relationship. Realizing this helped me to acknowledge that while I do have a real need for romantic love, as many people do, neither it nor even the traditional family is the exclusive or singular source of lasting and ultimate social fulfillment. In fact, the traditional belief in the supremacy of the nuclear family, among various kinds of social units, is one of the primary tools with which rulers keep us in subjugation.

Jesus says precisely this in one of his most radical teachings: "If anyone comes to me and does not hate father and mother, wife and children, brothers and sisters—yes, even their own life—such a person cannot be my disciple. And whoever does not carry their cross and follow me cannot be my disciple."[6] Oof. Yikes, Jesus. Hate our families and ourselves? Aren't you always telling us to hate no one and love everyone?

Jesus is using very strong, seemingly self-contradictory language to make it clear to us that he's making one of the most radical statements he ever makes. What he's doing is showing the movement how to become unbreakable. Unfragmentable.

Jesus is definitely abolishing something in this statement. But he's not abolishing self-love or love for the people closest to us. He's not abolishing the family *qua* family; he's abolishing the *nuclear* family. He's abolishing the family *qua* tool of the state to keep people from radical living. The state knows that many people who would otherwise resist choose not to in order to protect or preserve their families.[7] Jesus is saying that for radicals (disciples, members of the movement), devotion to our families cannot take precedence over our devotion to the movement and to the beloved community.

Jesus is not abolishing the family. Family is a good gift from God. He's abolishing a distortion of that good gift—the nuclear family. He's

---

6. Luke 14:26–27. Paul is echoing this in 1 Corinthians 7 when he says, "I wish that all of you were as I am [single] . . . now to the unmarried and the widows I say: It is good for them to stay unmarried, as I do." Can't have nuclear families if everyone's single, but you can have a bunch of really beautiful different alternative kinship structures. There was actually a very strong current in the early church that rejected marriage and sex entirely, for this reason. Many pockets of the early church really did abolish the nuclear family.
7. Melissa Florer-Bixler is spot on about this in her book *How to Have an Enemy: Righteous Anger and the Work of Peace* (Harrisonburg, VA: MennoMedia, 2021).

saying we need to start building the kind of communities in which no one kinship unit thinks of itself as ultimate or self-sufficient.

Abolishing the nuclear family means that no one person is solely responsible for the survival of anyone else. We're doing away with primary providers.

Abolishing the nuclear family means replacing the individual family economy in which one or two people are obligated to provide for the needs of the family and those of no one else, with mutual aid systems by which the community as a whole, not the family, is the be-all and end-all for having individuals' needs met.

And this is exactly what the church in Jerusalem does. There is a variety of kinship units, including families, but there are no nuclear families and certainly no primary financial providers. Everyone contributes according to ability, and everyone receives according to need. Distribution is arranged communally. There is no private property, which means there are no families who consider their possessions and resources to be exclusively their own.

The word *nucleus* means "the central and most important part of an object, movement, or group, forming the basis for its activity and growth." Thus the concept of the nuclear family is the idea that the family is the central and most important part of a person's larger social network. Which seems correct, right? I feel like not many people would argue with that if you said exactly that sentence to them. Dom Toretto certainly wouldn't.[8]

This is actually a regressive concept.

The family is good. But seeing the family as a community unto itself, as self-sufficient, is a mistake. It's a shortsighted form of socialization that inevitably causes fragmentation and chauvinism.

---

8. I've actually never seen any of the *Fast and Furious* movies but they're such a part of the zeitgeist that I reference them regularly.

It's just like nationalism; in fact, it's a smaller-scale model of the same thing. The idea of organizing socially around people with whom we share a common life, history, and/or heritage—communalism—is fine and natural and good. But when that dynamic becomes fixed, static, exclusionary, and noncooperative, it becomes regressive.

If we abolished borders, chauvinism, and competition between people groups, we wouldn't have nations anymore. We'd just have communities cooperating in a decentralized form (confederalism). Similarly, if we abolished the "borders" of kinship (i.e., you can only be part of my family, my closest kinship unit, if I love you romantically, or if I gave birth to you and/or am raising you, or if we're immediately related by blood) and the chauvinism of the nuclear family (I will choose my family even over ethics, the movement, the community, etc.), we wouldn't have *nuclear* families anymore. Families would not be the nucleus. They'd be one of many neutrons and protons that make up the nucleus—the community—along with friendships and other kinship structures.

A much simpler way to put it is that our communal forms always have to be subject to ethics and logic. Family is good, but having a deeper love—we're talking *agape* love here, not *eros* or *philia*—for certain people over others is unethical. And trying to make the nuclear family into a freestanding, self-sufficient social unit is illogical.

decentering the family and decentralizing kinship

In an anarchic community, one person being martyred, God forbid, would not mean the desolation of, say, one to four people who utterly depend on that person for their survival. The state could no longer neutralize us simply by picking one out of every four people and merely threatening them with imprisonment or murder. In the movement, the idea of organizing ourselves in a way that makes it easy for rulers to do that will be a ludicrous thing of the past. The state would have to destroy the entire community in order to neutralize us. But they wouldn't be able to do that because then who would they live off of?

If the people organized at a critical mass, we would be unstoppable because for the state to stop us would literally be to spell its own demise. Without us to fill their police forces, military ranks, tax coffers, and production and distribution jobs—for slave wages that allow them to live off of self-replenishing surplus—they would die, probably literally but certainly figuratively as a ruling class who by definition exists in a parasitic relationship with the people.

This is what it means to become ungovernable.[9] It's about becoming unexploitable, unrulable, unco-optable, unbreakable, like Kimmy Schmidt. It's about organizing so cooperatively that we cannot be fragmented. It's about making zero compromises with the logic of rulers.

It's about revealing deeper and subtler ways that we have adopted the logic of the state and rejecting them in increasingly radical ways. In this case, it's about realizing that it's not just patriarchy or heterarchy that we must root out but rather even the nuclear family as a regressive way to organize ourselves socially.

This is what made the early church undefeatable until it allowed itself to be co-opted by Rome. They were violently repressed but nonetheless ungovernable. There was no way for the ruling class to find the "core" of the movement and destroy it. There *was* no core. There were no rulers. There were no pockets of statist logic or organization that could be exploited, but if there were, they were *immediately* done away with (e.g., the logic/ethics of Ananias and Sapphira).

---

9.   This is a common anarchist slogan. I'm trying to get "obsolesce the state!" or simply "obsolesce!" going, but I gotta admit, they're not quite as catchy.

There were no weak spots. "You can throw some of us in prison, but that doesn't affect our organizational structure at all. You can martyr Stephen, but we don't fall apart without him—he's not our ruler. You can banish us with violence, but we'll just organize in other places. We will not be governed. We will not compromise."

And yet today, we allow ourselves to be bamboozled. Hood-winked. Led astray. Run amok. Every *Fast and Furious* movie, every rom-com—we are constantly bombarded by messaging that centers and elevates the nuclear family, and we eat it all up. No crumbs.

Again, I'm not saying that people are not going to naturally have deeper friendships with the people they spend the most time with or are not going to be particularly close with people they have romantic connections with or people they have given birth to and/or raised. Families are a good thing! But to make them nuclear (central, higher, ultimate) is to adopt the logic of the state and play right into frag-mentation and chauvinism. The *way* we practice family-making in our culture is unethical and irrational.

Statecraft would ideally like us to all be pure individualists who believe that the only people we can rely on are ourselves. That would be the ultimate fragmentation. But alongside this, and as a next resort—that is, the next most fragmented social unit—it hopes to make us believe that the nuclear family is our only real solace in the midst of a chaotic, evil world and that we can't ultimately rely on people who aren't bonded to us by immediate progeny or marriage. This is the same thing they do with original sin but even subtler—they create a cultural principle that both obscures and shifts the blame for the fragmentation that they, in fact, have created, making it seem natural and inevitable and justifying the policies they create to uphold and manage it.

The potency of the nuclear family for co-optation lies precisely in its intrinsic goodness. It is *good* to fall in love, to take vows to other people, to nurture young people, to go through the ups and downs of life together, etc. So to co-opt that very good thing and to ever so subtly distort it into something regressive is an extremely effective tactic. But the good news is that we never have to let ourselves be co-opted.

We can call out the state's appropriation of family for what it is and refuse to relate to our families in a nuclear way. We can encourage the proliferation of all kinds of kinship units and hold them in equal esteem. We can live by mutual aid systems that socialize and collectivize our meeting of all of our needs. We can anarchize all of our relationships.

conclusion

What I love about anarchy is that it allows us to get to 201- and 301-level ethical issues like these. What's the most liberative way to practice family-making? What is the most virtuous and freeing way to build relationships? Without anarchy, we remain permanently stuck on the 101—really 001—questions. Is it okay to exploit people? Should poverty exist? Should women be treated as equal to men? Should a small group of people be allowed to hoard 99 percent of power and resources?

Anarchy does not resolve all social questions. It simply allows us to advance higher and higher through them rather than taking two ethical steps forward, one step back, one step forward, three steps back.

Nine

clock's end

anarchy in eschatology

One recent summer I served as the chaplain (speaker) at a christian camp. I got to walk seventy kids through Jesus's Sermon on the Mount. Most adults, including me, find these teachings extremely difficult—first to grasp, then to follow. How in the world was I supposed to introduce them to kids ages eight through eighteen? "Do not worry." How am I supposed to pull that off? "Turn the other cheek." And be a doormat?

For the latter, I had to figure out a way to explain that Jesus, in peak anarchist form, is talking about nonviolent resistance and dramatized direct action. That it's neither about giving in nor getting even but rather about giving love. Not love as a sentimental feeling toward one's oppressor but rather as an extension of one's own humanity to the humanity in them. Confronting them with the confounding experience of seeing someone respond to hatred with resolve and dignity rather than acquiescence or vengeance. Dramatizing the injustice by doing something unexpected—namely, rejecting both acquiescence and vengeance—which calls all the more attention to the power of an empathic framework oriented toward the humanity (feelings and needs) in all of us.

I used the example of John Lewis. How he was trained for the sit-ins and the freedom rides by studying the Sermon on the Mount. He learned to love his enemies by affirming their humanity through the action of dramatically confronting them with his own. And if John Lewis and the freedom fighters could change reality through dramatic, nonviolent, nonretributive confrontation with systems of harm, how much more can God?

Eschatology is belief about the end times. It is my favorite area of theology. I love reading what the scriptures say about the escha- ton, and reading between the lines, and thinking about how to make our current world more like the world to come.

Christian eschatology is anarchy. It is the ethical union of all people, governing themselves under the loving care of God.

Yes, *all people*. That's crucial to the ethics of the gospel, which is why Paul says that God will reconcile *all* things to themself through Jesus. I believe God will do it. All things. All of creation. God will accomplish this through an irresistible story that we cannot help but be swept up in, through the all-consuming dramatization of their own glory and goodness.

the traditional eschatology of judgment

In chapter 4, I laid out an argument for why it is more fruitful to think in terms of harm than in terms of sin. And throughout this book I've rejected punishment as a means of addressing harm and instead appealed to restoration based on the meeting of all parties' needs.

So you might imagine that I do not believe in a hell that exists as a punishment for those who die without having their "sins" forgiven by God.

However, I do believe in a place where those who freely choose to reject love have it revealed to them for the beautiful thing that it is. I believe that there is strong support for such an eschatology in scripture, even though there were certainly many in biblical times that received God's revelation as presenting a place of eternal punitive incarceration.

purgation

Many of the greatest church fathers and mothers, including Irenaeus, the Cappadocian fathers, Athanasius, Origen, Clement, etc., believed that any discipline inflicted by God is therapeutic and cathartic, not retributive or punitive. Therefore, they saw hell not as *punishment for* one's sins but rather as *purgation of* one's sins over an amount of time proportional to one's sins, for the purpose of eventual restoration unto the presence and family of God.

Many of these same people also believed in a doctrine called the harrowing of hell. Much of the early church taught that between Good Friday and Easter, Jesus went down to hell, preached to the people there, and then liberated hell, bringing everyone out with him on his way out.

My eschatology takes cues from these teachings, as well as from all the scriptures that seem to be teaching universal restoration, which we'll go over shortly. Just as I see this life as containing realms where God is repairing harm in many ways, I see the next life as containing realms where God repairs harm in similar ways.

Within our tradition there has been a belief in a place called Sheol, there has been a belief in a place called Hades, and there has been a belief in a place called Hell. I wonder if there is room in our tradition for a belief in a place that goes by these names, or some other name, but is understood differently. A place where God cares for people through a process of next-worldly harm repair. A process that is therapeutic and cathartic, oriented toward purging people of the mindsets, habits, and everything within them which prevents them from treating themselves and others with empathy. A process wherein they are refined by a God who is a consuming fire of love.

We've bifurcated this one earth into two worlds, have we not?

One of those worlds is hellish. A place where harm is defined in a way that puts us more and more out of touch with our humanity, where the response to harm is punishment, where people are burned in the fires of the gods, gods which masquerade as YHWH but are in fact images of Satan, to whom the gods Mammon and Moloch answer. A place where people are tormented unendingly. A place where people seek to prevent harm by appealing to a statist system that actually creates and perpetuates harm.

The other world is heavenly. It's a place where the response to harm is empathy that acknowledges the humanity in our harm and connects it to the humanity in our healing. A place where people relate to one another out of solidarity, cooperation, freedom, and love. A place where harm is repaired through reformation and restoration.

Who was it that made this one earth into two separate worlds? Surely not God? It was human beings, was it not?

We've done the same thing with the new earth. We've taken one eschatological earth and divided it into two realms.

One we've fashioned in the image of the hell that already exists on this earth. A realm whose framework for harm response admits no vision other than incarceration and punishment.

The other realm we've often fashioned according to all the hopes, dreams, visions, relationships, dynamics, structures, and systems that we have allowed ourselves to believe we can't build here and now. A realm we often view through a lens of unspeakable fantasy and magic because our impaired imaginations are unable to picture a utopia that is built through the non-fantastic, non-magical, natural means of cooperation, solidarity, and anarchy.

We appeal to the cosmic state to disappear the people we judge as unworthy of the good life, and we appeal to the cosmic state to bestow upon us the good life we're more than capable of building ourselves, under the caring guidance of the Spirit. We forget that Jesus *came*—past tense—that we may have life, and life more abundantly.

We've taken this earth and divided it into heaven and hell. And we've done the same with the earth to come.

I would love to see us abolish both borders. I would love to see us fashion, theologically, all aspects of the next earth in the image of the world that God created and Jesus recreated. To see eschatological harm repair as occurring through loving reformation and restoration. To see the fire of God as a bright light that illuminates. Illuminates the beauty in us so that we can escape destructive shame and embrace generative grief. Illuminates our true feelings and needs so that we can then identify the best ways to express and meet them. Illuminates the feelings and needs of others so that we can seek to care for them out of love.

Humans have certainly created hell on earth, and we have certainly conceived of the next life in the same hellish ways. Ultimately, however, there is no place in the universe, in the multiverse, in existence that is not enveloped by God's care. Where the Spirit is, there is freedom. Where Christ is, there is heaven. And where are they absent? The Spirit is everywhere. God permeates all of God's creation. No person and no thing can exist outside of God, and if God is love, there is no place in which God is not actively loving.

We create hell but God goes on creating heaven. We create hell but God harrows our hells. Every hell we create gets harrowed by Jesus Christ. He purges the hell within us. He decimates the hell outside of us.

My deep conviction is that the place we call hell is a place where God gives us infinite chances to respond to them, where God preaches love to us even after our death, and where God's presence eventually becomes so brilliantly apparent that it will be impossible to be deceived by anything that purports to meet our needs without doing so through solidarity.

universalistic texts

So if any and all eschatological "fire" is purgative, therapeutic, cathartic, illuminating, liberating, and restorative, now we can make sense of so many other texts that have never seemed to match up quite right with the ones about exclusion and punishment:

- "And when I am lifted up from earth, I will drag all people to myself."[1]
- "You have entrusted him with every human being, that he may give eternal life to every being that you have given him. Eternal life is that they know you."[2]
- "Heaven must keep him until the times of the restoration of all beings."[3]
- "Because of one human being condemnation has spread to all humans. Likewise, thanks to the work of justice of one human being life-giving justification pours upon all humans. By virtue of the obedience of one human, all will be made just."[4]
- "'As I live,' says the Lord, 'every knee shall bow to me, and every tongue shall give praise to God.'"

---

1. John 12:31–32.
2. John 17:1–2.
3. Acts 3:20–21.
4. Romans 5:18–19.

- "Every knee will bow . . . and every tongue proclaim that Jesus Christ is the Lord."[5]
- "As all humans die in Adam, so will all humans be made alive in Christ."[6]
- "God will be all in all."[7]
- "For Christ also suffered for sins once for all, the righteous for the unrighteous, in order to bring you to God. He was put to death in the flesh, but made alive in the spirit, in which also he went and made a proclamation to the spirits in prison, who in former times did not obey. . . . For this is the reason the gospel was proclaimed even to the dead, so that, though they had been judged in the flesh as everyone is judged, they might live in the spirit as God does."[8]

Really rounds things out, doesn't it? Funny how these texts don't get preached nearly as much, isn't it? It's almost as if our suppositions shape our reading of the text just as much as the text shapes our worldview.

The late Rachel Held Evans said it well—when it comes to the Bible, you're going to find what you're looking for.[9] If you're looking for determinism, you'll find it. If you're looking for libertarianism

---

5. Philip 2:10–11. This verb for *bow* in greek always implies a *voluntary* recognition. These are not conquered resistors begrudgingly bowing. These are the rescued and redeemed, bowing out of grateful reverence.
6. 1 Corinthians 15:22–23.
7. 1 Corinthians 15:28.
8. 1 Peter 3:18–20; 4–6.
9. "We all go to the text looking for something, and we all have a tendency to find it . . . if you are looking for Bible verses with which to support slavery, you will find them. If you are looking for verses with which to abolish slavery, you will find them. If you are looking for verses with which to oppress women, you will find them. If you are looking for verses with which to honor and celebrate women, you will find them . . . if you are looking for an outdated and irrelevant ancient text, that's exactly what you will see. If you are looking for truth, that's exactly what you will find." Rachel Held Evans, *Inspired: Slaying Giants, Walking on Water, and Loving the Bible Again* (Nashville: Thomas Nelson, 2018), 56–57.

(free will), you'll find it. If you're looking for an inherent sinfulness that will not be extricated from human nature until the eschaton, you'll find it. If you're looking for genuine unassailable human goodness, you'll find it. If you're looking for an eternal, punitive hell, you'll find it. If you're looking for universal salvation, you'll find that too. When it comes to eschatology, what are we looking for?

Friends, I know the sum total of what I'm proposing here is a radical theological departure. A Christ who didn't need to die on the cross. A Messiah who didn't need to "take our place" and be punished for the "transgressions" we committed. A Jesus who didn't come to "save us from our sin" so much as to show us what liberation looks like—like a mustard seed, like leaven, like a treasure hidden in a field—and to work alongside us to get everyone free—organizing, teaching, healing, renewing, and sending people out to do the same. A hell that was always heaven, always a place of restoration. It's a big theological remodel.

If you're like me, you may even wonder if this is a completely different Jesus. It's like finding out you've been mispronouncing your best friend's name for years, or that this whole time they've had a rad birthmark that you've never noticed.

Jesus can handle it. He's been millions of different things to millions of different people. Our understanding of him not only can but also should evolve over the course of our relationship with him. Isn't that how relationships work?

I'm the same person I was ten years ago, and yet I'm a completely different person than I was ten years ago. The same can be said for the Jesus I know and love. He's a liberator in ways that I never knew. He went onto and off of the cross in some ways that I never knew. He came out of the grave in ways that I never knew. He's in the world now in ways that I never knew. He's the object of my worship in ways that I never knew. He's God in ways that I never knew.

He's still Jesus though! He's still the image of the invisible! He's still the face of the unfathomable! He's still the tactility of the intangible! He's still the expression of the ineffable! He's still the usher of the unimaginable! He's still the one in whom and through whom all things were created! He's still the one from whom all things follow and in whom all things hold together! He's still the love of my life. He's still God.[10]

The riches of the glory of this mystery are nothing more and nothing less than Christ in us, the hope of glory. All things in Jesus, Jesus in all things. All people are in ethical union with God and co-caretaking with God and participation in God. A union that invites us further up and further into God's inexhaustible glory:

> And thus are those who have stood by God who glorified them, they persevere, astounded by the excess of glory, and by the endless addition of divinity's splendor. For the end will be eternal progress, the condition of additional, endless fulfillment, and shall make an attainment of the Unattainable, and God of whom no one can get enough, shall become the source of satisfaction for all.

> But the full measure of God and the glory of their light will be an abyss of progress, and an endless beginning . . . how, tell me, would they grasp the end of the endless? It is impossible and by all means impracticable . . . their perfection shall be endless, and the progress shall be everlasting.[11]

---

10. Go back and read this paragraph again, but this time insert a Black church organ hit in between each sentence.
11. Symeon the New Theologian, tenth-century Byzantine abbot, speaking about *epektasis*, the doctrine of everlasting progress.

Ten

work in progress
anarchy in action

Even though this book is a systematic theology manifesto, I can't leave y'all without pointing to at least a couple of practical examples of anarchy in action. Before I do that, though, let me say a few things as a preface.

First, I hope I've clearly expressed that anarchy is a sociologically narrow-to-broad, simple-to-compound movement. It is a deeply *localistic* philosophy, centered on the municipality and extending its principles outward from there. As such, any sustainable anarchic movement is going to live primarily at the local level, with anarchic groups gradually transforming their communities. Regional and other nonlocal networks can surely share information and resources, coordinate actions, etc., but there will be no "national" anarchist "takeover" (an oxymoron), and there will be no regional-to-local progression of anarchy. Consequently, the examples I'm going to share are precisely this—small communities of people who are working to make the state obsolete and to take care of their own needs at the local level.

Second, none of these examples are groups of self-avowed anarchists. Nonetheless, they are groups of people who, whether identifying

WORK IN PROGRESS   153

as leftist, socialist, Black liberationist, or none of the above, are following the basic anarchic principles of cooperation, care, and equality. This
is one of the many things I love about anarchism—one does not need
to be a philosophical anarchist in order to work anarchically. Anarchism
is simply the systematic articulation of basic self-evident human principles, and therefore it need not be systematized to be practiced any
more than Newton's laws need to be scientifically articulated in order
for someone to understand how doors work.[1] Even if not driven by a
conscious desire to obsolesce the state, any ethical work that serves to
make the state obsolete does in fact do the work of anarchy.

It is unlikely that there will ever be a large-scale movement of
people who all consciously assent to a particular systematic philosophy.
But there have been, and again will be, movements driven by the basic
self-evident ethics of love, care, and cooperation. Ultimately, what matters in the end is not how well one grasps the "best" ideas, but how well
one loves.[2] So let me reiterate that I'm categorizing the following groups
and projects as anarchic not because they have a self-conscious anarchist philosophy but rather because they operate according to principles
of autonomous community care and self-provision, equity, cooperative
decision-making, and/or, most importantly, providing alternatives to
services and structures ostensibly provided by the state.

Okay, let's get into it! These are groups in or near my local context in New Jersey, which is the main context I'd feel positioned to
comment on.

---

1.   This is actually a great way to think of anarchism. Just as Newton's laws,
      according to legend, come from his experience of getting hit by an apple falling
      out of a tree, so can the principles of anarchism arise out of the natural, every-
      day experiences of human beings who intuitively believe in love and coopera-
      tion. Anarchism is simply the systematic articulation and extension of those
      intuitive beliefs into a comprehensive worldview.
2.   "Dear friends, let us love one another, for love comes from God. Everyone who
      loves has been born of God and knows God" (1 John 4:7).

restorative justice hubs

I have interacted here and there with a New Jersey–based collective called Salvation and Social Justice. They recently launched a restorative justice hub, the first of its kind in New Jersey, which works to divert folks in the Trenton community away from the "justice" system of the state and instead toward a community-based process for addressing and repairing harm.

While there are several philosophies and toolkits out there for restorative justice groups to base their work on, the organization *Impact Justice* has a *Restorative Justice Project* that helpfully lays out the principles and methods that organizations like Salvation and Social Justice use. They start out by making clear that they are working to "shift the paradigm from seeing crime as a violation of the law to understanding crime as harm that requires individual, interpersonal, community, and system-wide support for accountability and healing."[3] They seek to achieve healthy outcomes for youth accused of crime *and* to meet the self-identified needs of people harmed.

How does restorative justice do this? Let me first share their overview of the process, and then I'll share the more detailed rundown.[4]

restorative justice overview

When an instance of interpersonal harm takes place in the community, instead of sending the case to the police and courts, the person

---

3. This is a big tenet of anarchist conflict mediation. We do not allow the state/rulers to determine what harm is. "Crime" is what the state has decided harm is; it's a label they can apply to anything that threatens their rulership. Anarchists remove the word *crime* from our vocabulary, instead speaking of harm and harm repair in a way that is not referential to the state but rather to our communities.

4. This is all taken from the website of the Restorative Justice Project of the organization Impact Justice: https://rjdtoolkit.impactjustice.org/establish -a-foundation/restorative-justice-diversion/.

harmed (PH) and their support network can instead send the case to a community-based restorative organization. The person responsible (PR) is asked to consent to the restorative process, which hopefully they do, if for no other reason, in recognition of its vast superiority to the apparatus of the police and prisons.[5] After the PH and the PR both consent to the process, they join together in a restorative community conference, also called a *peace circle*. The intent of the peace circle is to identify the needs of everyone—the PH, the PR, their supporters (family, friends, mentors, social workers, etc.), and the broader community—and to craft and agree to a plan for harm repair and personal restoration. After the peace circle, the community, particularly the supporters of the PH and PR, assist the latter in following through with the restorative plan, which leads, of course, to positive outcomes.

That's a quick overview of the process. The Restorative Justice Project provides a more detailed look at the process in three stages: preparation, conference, and plan completion. I've adapted it a bit, but I'm staying quite close to their description.

preparation

1. Build a relationship with the PR. Once they've agreed to participate in the restorative process, facilitators can spend time building a holistic relationship of trust and care with them, getting to know the whole of who they are, including

---

5. What if they refuse accountability? In an anarchist framework, to refuse the mediation of the community is to refuse to be a member of that community. To abolish rulers is to reify the cooperative power of the people, whereas to refuse to recognize the latter *is* to buy into the former. Such a person has voluntarily removed themselves from the community. "Let them be as a pagan or tax collector to you" (Matt. 5:17)—let them make their choice! But after the revolution, why would anyone freely do this?

their skills, motivations, opportunities, and interests, which they'll later incorporate into the plan for repair.

2. Have the PR reflect on the harm encounter, both their own experience and the impact of their actions on the PH and on the community.

3. Help the PR write an apology letter.

4. Build a relationship with the PH.

5. Prepare the PH and the PR for the peace circle over a series of meetings by explaining the process, identifying support people, helping them craft what they'd like to say, and so on.

6. Reach out to community members and the support people for both PR and PH and prep them for the peace circle, including by explaining the expectations for a support person in a peace circle.[6]

7. Coordinate logistical needs for the peace circle. Facilitators arrange for a confidential, a neutral, and an accessible space for the conference. They schedule it on a time and date that works for everyone. They provide food that meets everyone's dietary needs. They beautify the space.

conference / peace circle

1. Facilitators begin the meeting by welcoming everyone, honoring the Indigenous people of the land, and laying out the purpose, process, and intended outcome of the peace circle.

---

6. Of course, in some instances it will not be immediately clear who is the PH and who is the PR. In this instance, the support group for each person, along with the community, might listen and make a decision on how to proceed. In some instances, two or more people may be both responsible for harm *and* recipients of harm. In this case, we might apply both sides of the process to all relevant persons.

2. The PR reads their apology letter.
3. The PH shares how the harm impacted them. They can also ask questions to the PR about the harm.
4. The PR shares about the harm and responds to the PH's questions.
5. Support people for both persons, as well as community members, share how the harm has impacted them. They can ask questions of either person at this time.
6. Once everyone has had an opportunity to share, participants work together to craft a plan, by consensus, for the PR to make things right. The plan will likely involve expectations not only of the PR but also of their support system. The plan is based on the needs of all participants and uses goals that are specific, measurable, attainable, realistic, and time-framed (SMART).
7. Facilitators lead a closing ceremony once the plan has been crafted and expectations have been outlined.

plan completion

1. Facilitators and support networks help the PR identify and take steps toward completion of the restorative/reparative plan. They provide resources and guidance toward this end.
2. Supporters follow up with the PR periodically to check in on progress. If changes need to be made to the plan, facilitators help with that.
3. Once the PH, along with their supporters, has agreed that the plan has been accomplished, facilitators will arrange a closing meeting and celebration to mark the end of the process. The PH is welcome to attend if they would like to.

reflections

The Restorative Justice Project reports that these methods have led to a 91 percent satisfaction rate for persons harmed and a 44 percent reduction in recidivism for youth. And of course zero dollars wasted on legal fees, bail, and other ways of putting our money into the hands of the state. Resources, time, energy, and, most importantly, *people* stay in the community instead of being sent off to be punished and/or disappeared by rulers.

Again, I'm not aware of any restorative justice workers who are self-avowed anarchists. And yet Salvation and Social Justice is an organizing group rooted in the tradition of the Black church, which has always had to create alternative institutions to obsolesce the statist and white supremacist institutions that have either ignored us, at best, or actively harmed us. This is true of the Black church itself, of course, but also of Black mutual aid, Black innovation, Black neighborhoods, Black art, Black sports, and so on and so forth. So while there are certainly strong reformist currents within the Black liberation movement, I would argue that Black struggle has, and always has had, fundamentally anarchic elements within it. Restorative justice programs are one example of us taking care of ourselves, knowing that rulers neither want to nor can. It is an active outpouring of the recognition we've always had—that the state is obsolete.

The Restorative Justice Project has detailed instructions and resources to help people start restorative justice programs in their area. This is something well within our reach, right now, to do.

the Black Community Watchline of New Jersey

In 2020, a few friends and former educators of mine were part of the founding of the Black Community Watchline of New Jersey. In the organization's words, it was "created to empower individuals to speak out and address instances of anti-Black violence, aggression and bias" and to provide "a platform to report immediate threats of racial violence, microaggressions, and racially motivated experiences that undermine the respect, dignity and fair treatment that Black people should receive."[7]

The watchline currently encourages folks to call in the following instances:

- Anti-Black violent attack: use of physical force to harm a Black person with impunity[8]
- Racial profiling: Black person(s) being unfairly targeted based on negative assumed behaviors and stereotypes associated with Black presence
- Police encounter or weaponizing law enforcement: a Black person subjected to profiling, harassment, intimidation, and/or use of force by police or an unjustified racially motivated "suspicious person" 911 call due to Black presence in public or private spaces
- Institutions or industries: incidences of racial prejudice and discriminatory behaviors, practices, and/or actions within institutions or industries (e.g., being automatically assigned to a remedial class or receiving inferior medical care)

---

7. https://www.blackcommunitywatchline.com/about-black-community-watchline.
8. They go on to say that "calling 911 is a necessary and appropriate response to a hateful attack . . . a call to the Black Community Watchline in addition to calling 911 is a means of requesting support in dealing with the incident and navigating interaction with law enforcement." An anarchist/abolitionist, would, of course, reject all forms of dependence on and/or cooperation with the police.

- Whistleblower: an individual exposing illegal or unethical racialized activity or information from within a public or private organization
- Other

Now, let's be clear—a quick look at their policy platform reveals this is very much a reformist organization, not an abolitionist organization. And that's okay. This illustrates that reformists and abolitionists—people of various, even contradictory, philosophical leanings—can work together on meaningful projects of liberation. The work of anarchists and the work of reformists can sometimes overlap, largely because particular social actions can be interpreted in different ways. In the case of the watchline, I find a pretty strong basis for my interpretation of the project as coming from a mentality of having given up on the police to competently handle Black folks' needs to be heard, to document harm done to them, and to widen the circle of accountability. Of course, a police obsolescence or police abolition platform on its own is not enough to ensure a just society as police are merely one of the many tools of the state, which is itself the institutionalization of oppression, but it certainly can be a micro-anarchic political philosophy. I mean, I became an anarchist only when I connected the dots between my mini-anarchisms—that is, when I realized that the abolitionism that I had applied to various tools of the state needed to be applied to the head of the beast[9] itself.

One thing I appreciate about the Black Community Watchline is its simplicity. It's not trying to do a hundred different things. It's just providing one discrete and discreet way for Black people to meet our own needs, knowing that the state cannot and will not. For

---

9. Yep, you got it—the "beast" in Revelation represents the state.

generations, Black people have had the deconstructive analysis that we can't call the police for anything and certainly not for a competent response to instances of anti-Black harm. The watchline is a constructive project that responds to that deconstructive analysis and builds something better in the place of that which we know is obsolete. That's exactly what anarchy is.

The watchline currently exists to take calls on instances of anti-Black harm, but it could quite easily be expanded into a hotline for all instances where Black people need to draw on the resources of the community for timely assistance. A lot of poor and marginalized people call 911 when in crisis, simply because they have no one else who can help immediately. And yet, of course, the first people 911 dispatches are police, who almost invariably exacerbate the crisis, not least because they're trained to see themselves as at war with people, not to help people. The Black Community Watchline already reflects an understanding of this—that cops are here to police us, not to help us. It would not be a leap at all to expand this analysis from the area of instances of racism into the broader area of crisis in general. We can have a team of care professionals, who are either compensated by the community or are volunteers, ready to respond when someone accidentally locks their kid in the car, when someone falls in their house and hurts themself, when someone is having a mental health crisis, and the like. This would be a constructive way to redirect all crisis intervention needs away from the state and toward our communities themselves.

As anarchists we don't need to burn down courthouses or legislate police out of existence—nor would doing so be consistent with anarchism, in which the ends must cohere with the means, which rules out violence as a tactic, and in which there is no legislative activity, which relies on the state to enforce it. We can make the "judicial" system obsolete by creating our own restorative justice and crisis intervention apparatuses.

violence intervention with the Paterson Healing Collective

One fine example of the latter is the hospital-based violence intervention program (HVIP) of the Paterson Healing Collective in New Jersey. This program was created in partnership with St. Joseph's Hospital in Paterson to provide support and intervention for survivors of violence. Rather than rely solely on the medical aid that health care can provide, HVIPs administer care on "multiple levels of the social ecology" (i.e., individual, interpersonal, communal, and societal), understanding that responding to violence with medical aid without also providing mental, emotional, and social care outside of the apparatus of the state does nothing to stem the tide of recidivism and retaliation.

HVIPs provide victims of violence with links to community-based services, mentoring, home visits, follow-up care, and long-term case management. They also work to identify and reduce risk factors, such as substance misuse and chronic unemployment, and promote protective factors such as social support, job readiness, and educational attainment.

HVIPs remove police and lawyers from violence and crisis intervention, instead entrusting the response to these situations to health care professionals and trained community members. The latter apply trauma-informed practices to step in during the "teachable moment"—or wake-up call, frequently—of hospital recovery. Several studies have demonstrated that individuals are particularly receptive to interventions that promote positive behavior change at these moments in health care settings. This is largely because during hospitalization, victims of violence often "find themselves at a crossroads: they can continue on the path they were on prior to their injury, seek retaliation for the violence committed against them, or turn their traumatic experience into a reason to take themselves out of 'the game'—altering their life course trajectory."[10]

HVIPs intervene precisely at this crossroads and provide persons with a path forward that leads away from both direct state violence (courts, police, prisons) and from that interpersonal violence, which is itself the adoption of the logic of the state (an eye for an eye, evil for evil, power and security sought via domination). They provide folks with a way to make the state, in either form, obsolete by choosing love in the form of cooperation, restoration, and nonviolence even in the face of repeated violence. Thereby, after a recovery period characterized by holistic, restorative care, a patient is released from the hospital with a support network and a plan for overall safety and growth.

Hospital-based intervention is just one important component of the Healing Collective's overall community-centered harm reduction program, which also includes mentoring with an eye toward achieving short-term goals, violence survivor support groups, counseling, conflict mediation programs, community walks, and community forums.

These community walks take place in neighborhood "hotspots," where org members bring information about resources and services to residents who live in statistically violence-prone locations. The walks also serve to connect org members with potential mentees and to provide neighborhood residents an opportunity to talk about their needs with a caring listener.

The community forums, or roundtables, are a facilitated community dialogue where community members, activists, service

10. The white paper of Health Alliance for Violence Intervention (HAVI), p. 6, https://www.thehavi.org/.

providers, and faith-based organizations come together for discourse and decisions on transformative and restorative solutions to community issues. A people's assembly making decisions by consensus on how the community will administer its own common life and resources—sounds familiar, doesn't it?

praxis

As we've noted, liberation initiatives do not have to be self-consciously anarchist in order to align with anarchic principles. An abolitionist and a reformist can certainly collaborate on a community watchline, a restorative justice program, or a violence intervention apparatus. Of course, they will think of these projects differently. So while philosophy is not the be-all and end-all for action, it is certainly part of praxis.

Within my first week of seminary, I had learned that *praxis* is the three-part process of experience, reflection on that experience, and action based on that reflection, which either constitutes or leads to a new experience that restarts the process from the beginning. A reformist and an abolitionist can certainly have similar experiences that result in similar actions. But our reflection is going to be different, and ultimately that difference in the middle portion of our respective praxes will cause our actions to diverge.

Two people might both have the *experience* of being failed by the judicial system, and their respective *reflections* might lead both of them to take the *action* of participating in a restorative justice program. But out of this new experience, one might reflect, "Wow, if only the judicial system could operate this way," while the other might reflect, "Wow, I guess we don't need the 'judicial' system anymore, now do we?" And now their subsequent actions may likely diverge. The former might launch a campaign to bring restorative principles into the judicial process, while the latter might launch a campaign to defund police and redirect those community funds into restorative justice programs in their municipality.

In other words, ultimately teleology[11] comes into play in a big way. Are we trying to stop gaps in an otherwise good dam? Or are we trying to create more gaps so that the dam will collapse given that it's actually serving to make sure only a small group of people get water while most of us get nothing?

This is why philosophy is helpful. Anarchism as a political philosophy is one powerful way to help people fully extend the logic of their values. I know a lot of people who believe in love, cooperation, and care. I also know a lot of people who haven't extended those values fully to the point of embracing Black liberation, LGBTQ+ liberation, women's liberation, and socialism (the liberation of people in general). I know a smaller subset of people who *have* made those extensions but haven't extended the logic of love to their analysis of the state itself, or perhaps they have but haven't encountered a philosophy that gives them a viable alternative to statecraft. And you know what? Sometimes the construction of that alternative can happen on a mostly intellectual basis—neat!—but most often that happens experientially. So I'm a fan of working with reformists on appropriately aligned projects in hopes that the *experience* of anarchy in action, as well as that of working with anarchists, will lead to new *reflection* that helps them to extend their values more fully and thus to take appropriate *action*.

the river and the waterfall

Lastly, let's distinguish between good work that makes the state obsolete and good work that does *not* do this. Let's take, for example,

---

11. A teleology is a vision for the long-term and the ultimate purposes, aims, ends, and resolution of a project.

good work such as refugee resettlement and affordable housing programs. Does this work contribute to making the state obsolete? No, not inherently.

Imagine a river that turns into rapids and then spills over into a waterfall. Refugee resettlement and affordable housing are a net catching people who have plummeted over the edge of the waterfall of nationalism and capitalism.[12] It's lifesaving work, but it doesn't do anything to resolve the danger of the waterfall itself.

Community-based restorative justice and crisis intervention, among other things, are a net placed upriver to keep people from getting to the edge of the waterfall in the first place. Currently they're a net we stretch out over the rapids, after people's lives have already begun to get tossed around. But the more we refine and broaden our theory and our practices—collectively, our praxis—the further upstream the net goes, even hopefully to the point where one day it is upriver of even the rapids.

After the revolution, people still experience interpersonal conflict. People still experience crises. There may even be very, very infrequent instances of violence. But our systems for addressing, resolving, and preventing these phenomena will be so intricate, effective, and widespread that the difference between their resolution then and now will be like the difference between writing a research paper in 2023 and writing the same paper in 1983. Same general principles, vastly superior tools.

Refugee resettlement and affordable housing programs are a *lifeline* for thousands of people. But they, by definition, are responses

---

12. That is, the inherent, inevitable crises of nationalism, namely war, which causes displacement and forced migration, as well as the inherent, inevitable crises of capitalism, in this case the monopolization of housing by the propertied class who eat up all available housing and dominate the development of new housing and use it as a commodity to produce profit rather than as a good with which to care for people.

to the crises of nationalism and capitalism. They cannot, by defini-tion, be ways to make capitalism and statecraft obsolete any more than the act of firefighting can make house fires obsolete. Now, can firefighters advise construction companies and housing residents on how to gradually make house fires obsolete through better construc-tion practices and residential practices? Absolutely. In that case, social workers have infinite, unique value to add to the conversation of how to abolish the state and capitalism. But the occurrence of those kinds of conversations relies on a particular philosophical moti-vation and underpinning, which is where anarchism comes in.

That being said, work that responds to the crises of capitalism and statecraft can still do what it can to move away from a charity model and toward a mutual aid model.[13] It can seek out people from the affected communities (e.g., refugees, folks living in affordable housing) to contribute to and even facilitate decision-making and administration of resettlement and housing programs. It can seek to find alternative sources of funding rather than rely solely on funding from the state, which of course always comes with state-reinforcing strings attached, and/or donors who are rich due to capitalism and who use charitable giving to remain rich through tax write-offs and farcical "foundations." This will allow the people doing the work to remove "eligibility requirements," expectations of "deliverables," and other criteria that make the work reinforce rather than undermine statist and capitalist logic.

Bottom-of-the-waterfall work can become more anarchic by choosing to make decisions by consensus and to move away from bureaucratic models of leadership. It can train folks from the affected groups to become experts in the fields. It can remain as

---

13. For more on this, check out *Mutual Aid* by Dean Spade, wherein he eviscerates the charity model.

multi-issue-focused as possible, seeking solidarity with other liberation groups. It can adopt an adversarial mindset toward statecraft and capitalism rather than a cooperative mindset. And so much more.

If an organization you're a part of mostly does bottom-of-the-waterfall work, I'd recommend two things: see how you all can make that work more abolitionist and see if your broader community can't add a bit of "upriver" work as well. Both are great ways to put anarchy into action.

epilogue

The state—that is, the professionalization and centralization of rulership—is made by the bourgeoisie and for the bourgeoisie. It wasn't made for us. The fact that it doesn't serve us means it's working exactly as designed. If we want to build a society that's designed for us, we have to abolish the state and replace it with something that *can be* built by and for us. We need humanly scaled, communally administered towns and cities in which all participate, and all collectively oversee every aspect of civic life and from which we can support and interact with other cities in a commune of communes.

There's nothing that logically or inherently prevents us from doing this. Not some presumed total depravity, not any presumed need for coercion or monopolized violence. In fact, far from precluding anarchy, logic demands it. Christianity, as I've argued, demands it. Our humanity demands it. The structures of violence, dominion, and death are arrayed against it, but the nature of God and the nature of their creation are for it and cannot ultimately be denied. Let's acknowledge and celebrate these deeper realities now and start to live in ways that increasingly reflect them.

In 1935, W. E. B. Du Bois published *Black Reconstruction*, a systematic socialist reinterpretation of not only a historical event but also of much of the cultural tradition that led to it and that which followed from it. It's long as heck, but it's rad. Everyone thought the story was settled, but Du Bois decided to take his training, his experience, and his perspective, as well as the voices of his ancestors and his community, into account in order to take another look. And even though social studies textbooks and college-level history syllabi to this day still regurgitate the narratives Du Bois sought to subvert, a fuller understanding is there for those who are looking for it.

I hope for this book to be a systematic anarchist reinterpretation of not only the historical events of Jesus Christ but also much of the cultural and spiritual tradition that set the stage for it and that which followed from it. I tried to replace Du Bois's long encyclopedic lists of facts, figures, and names with jokes—comic relief, am I right?— and I tried to shave off six hundred pages, but ultimately I hoped to accomplish something similar. Many think the story of christianity is settled, but history is full of homies who knew that it certainly was not. I'm here to stand on their shoulders—I'm used to this; I'm too short to be able to see at concerts—and honor them by building on what they did, just as I hope generations after me do with my work. And the cool thing is I don't need to take down the dominant narrative. All I hope to do is hasten its obsolescence.

This book is one person's anarchist theological system. As I mentioned, these are theological and political opinions, supported by evidence whose selection is very ideologically motivated. But I think I make a pretty solid case. The way I see it, christianity is anarchic, and so are its implications for what we believe about God, humanity, interaction between God and humanity, the Bible, church history, church administration, ethics, the end of this world, and the beginning of the next.

Thank you for reading and considering this proposal. I hope that you, like the bereans, go home and examine the scriptures—and your experience, and your reason, and the tradition, and your fellow believers, and the voice of the Holy Spirit—to see if these things are true.

Now, I ain't gon' hold you, but if you're thinking, "Okay, yes, what do I do now?" remember that it's not so much about joining anarchist organizations—although do that if you can!—as it is about anarchizing the work you already do and the relationships you're already in. Rejecting violence, coercion, domination, and rulership wherever they present themselves and setting an intention to build structures of care. Ultimately anarchy is merely the political dimension of love. Love is the answer. So with that in mind, let's get after it. For the culture. For the revolution. For each other. For love. For funsies. For Narnia. For Aslan.

> Then the LORD answered me and said:
> Write the vision;
> make it plain on tablets,
> so that a runner may read it.
>
> For there is still a vision for the appointed time;
> it speaks of the end, and does not lie.
> If it seems to tarry,[1] wait for it;
> it will surely come, it will not delay.[2]

---

1. If it seems to *terry*, am I right?
2. Habakkuk 2:2–3.

further reading

Ahrens, Gale, ed. *Lucy Parsons: Freedom, Equality and Solidarity— Writings and Speeches, 1878–1937.* Chicago: Charles H. Kerr, 2003.

Anderson, William C. *The Nation on No Map: Black Anarchism and Abolition.* Chico, CA: AK Press, 2021.

Bey, Marquis. *Anarcho-Blackness: Notes toward a Black Anarchism.* Chico, CA: AK Press, 2020.

Bookchin, Murray. *The Next Revolution: Popular Assemblies and the Promise of Direct Democracy.* London: Verso, 2015.

Christoyannopoulos, Alexandre. *Christian Anarchism: A Political Commentary on the Gospel.* Abridged ed. Exeter: Imprint Academic, 2013.

Daring, C. B., J. Rogue, Deric Shannon, Abbey Volcano, eds. *Queering Anarchism: Addressing and Undressing Power and Desire.* Chico, CA: AK Press, 2013.

Horsley, Richard A. *Jesus and Empire: The Kingdom of God and the New World Disorder.* Minneapolis: Fortress Press, 2003.

Parsons, Lucy, Lorenzo Kom'boa Ervin, Ashanti Alston, Kuwasi Balagoon, Sam Mbah, Michael Kimble, Pedro Ribeiro, et al. *Black Anarchism: A Reader by the Black Rose Anarchist Federation.* Chico, CA: AK Press, 2020.

Spade, Dean. *Mutual Aid: Building Solidarity during This Crisis (and the Next).* Brooklyn, NY: Verso, 2020.